AF334604

# Moms and Paws

Photos by Sandra Bolan
Edited by Jacque Newman and Brian Balogh

Published in 2007 by Fetch it Up!

www.fetchitup.ca

Library and Archives Canada Cataloguing in Publication
Bolan, Sandra

Moms and Paws: An intimate look at women and their best friends
Photography by Sandra Bolan
Edited by Jacque Newman and Brian Balogh
ISBN 978-0-9739737-1-6

1. Pets--Pictorial works. 2. Women--Pictorial works.
3. Pet owners--Pictorial works. 4. Human-animal relationships.
I. Balogh, Brian, II. Newman, Jacque, 1955- III. Title.
SF416.5.B64 2007     636.088'70222     C2007-901058-X

*"I gave my beauty and my youth to men.*

*I am going to give my wisdom and experience*

*- the best of me -  to animals."*

*- Brigitte Bardot*

Georgie stole my heart when she

was no bigger than my hand.

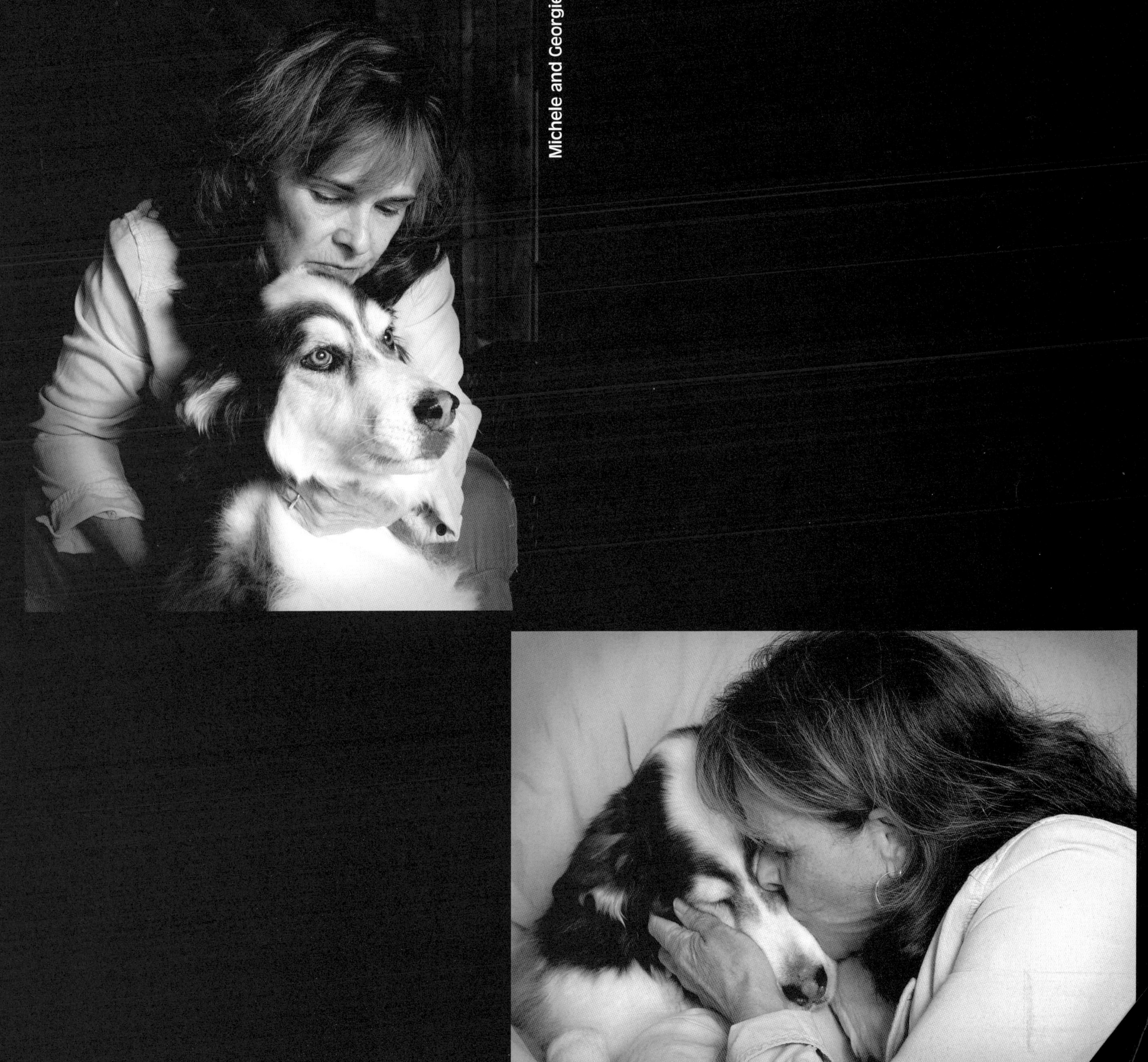
Michele and Georgie

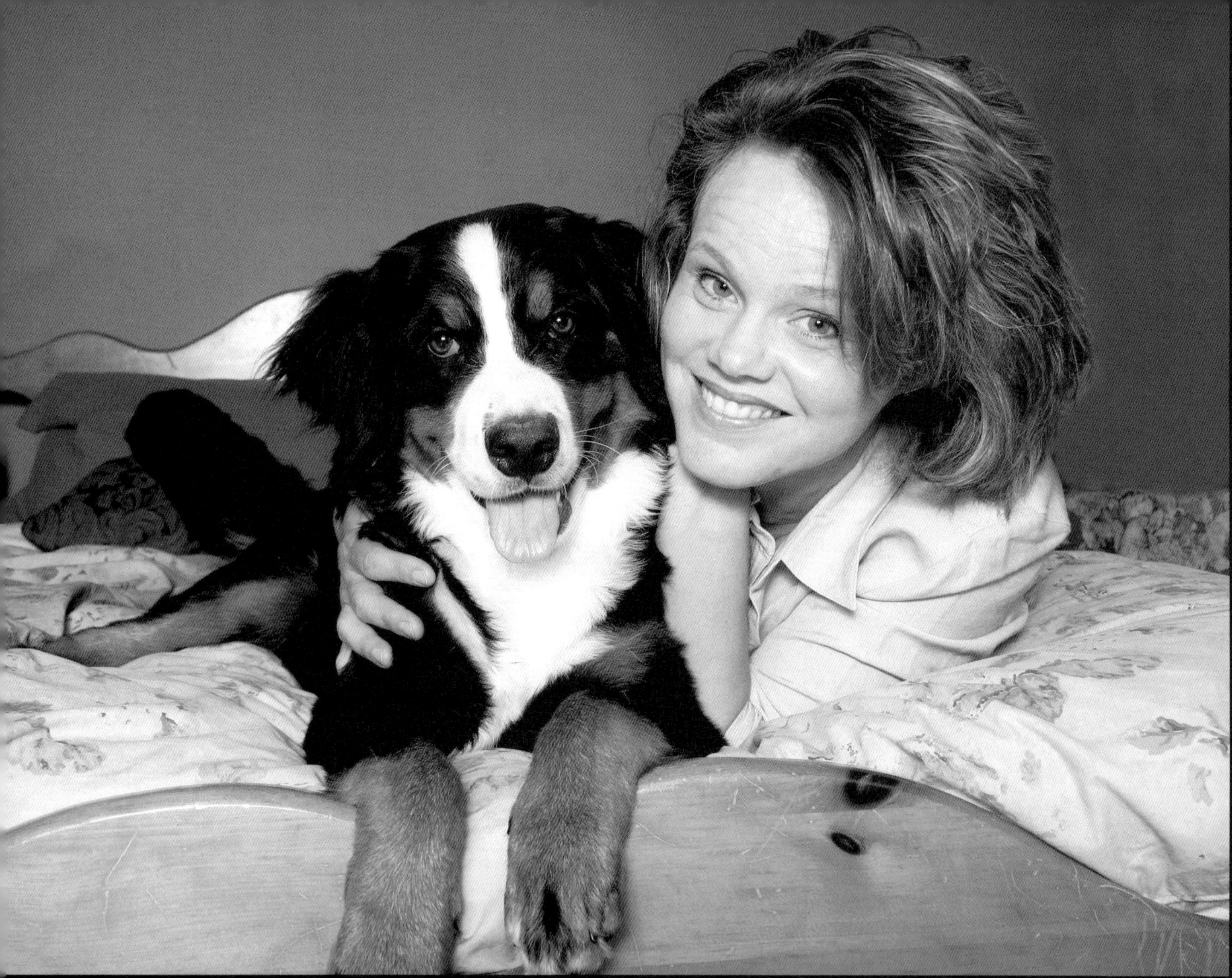

Heidi and I have been together just a short time
but she's already wriggled her way into my heart.

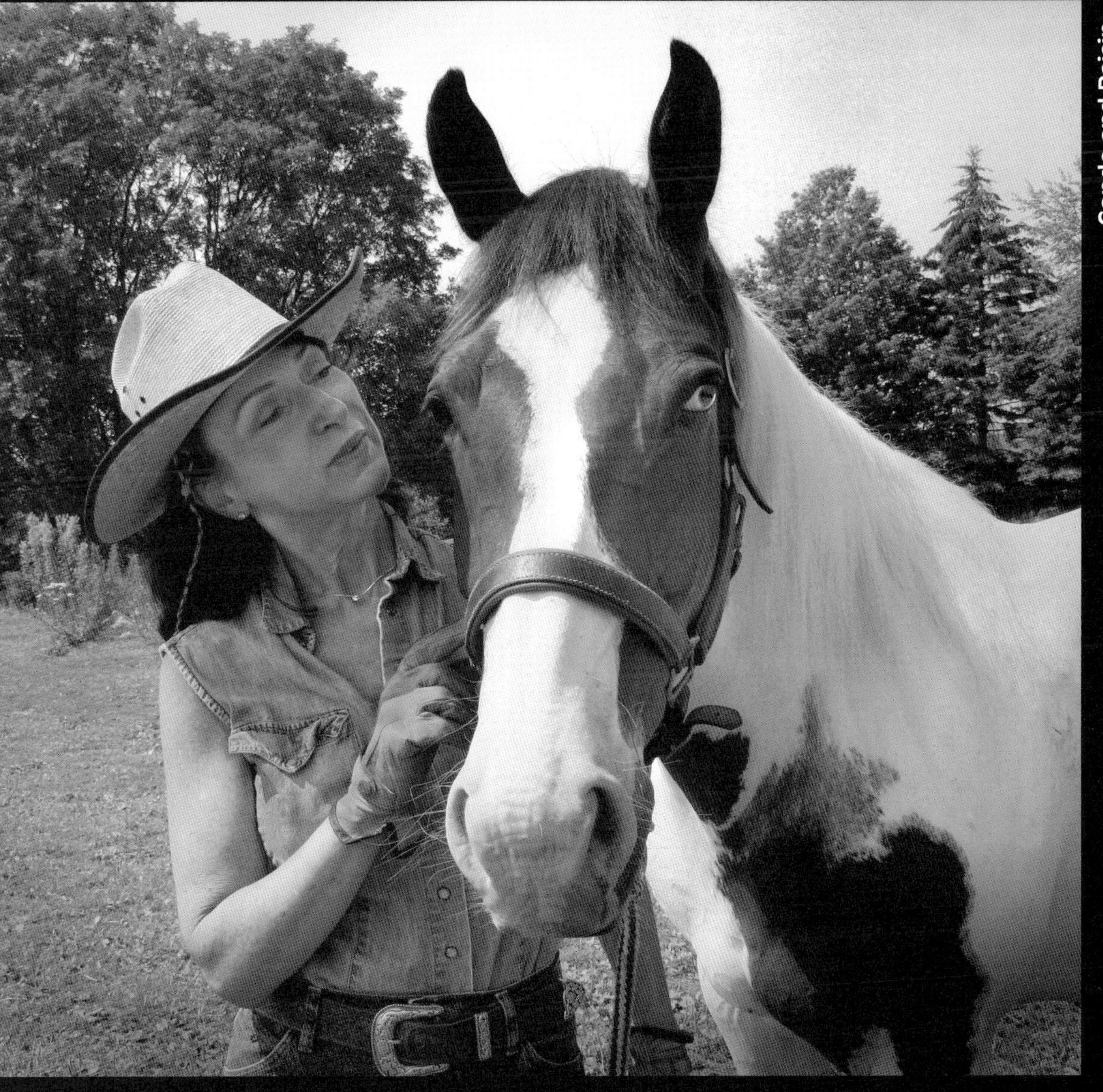


He often comes when I call him

but only when he feels like it and if he's not grazing,

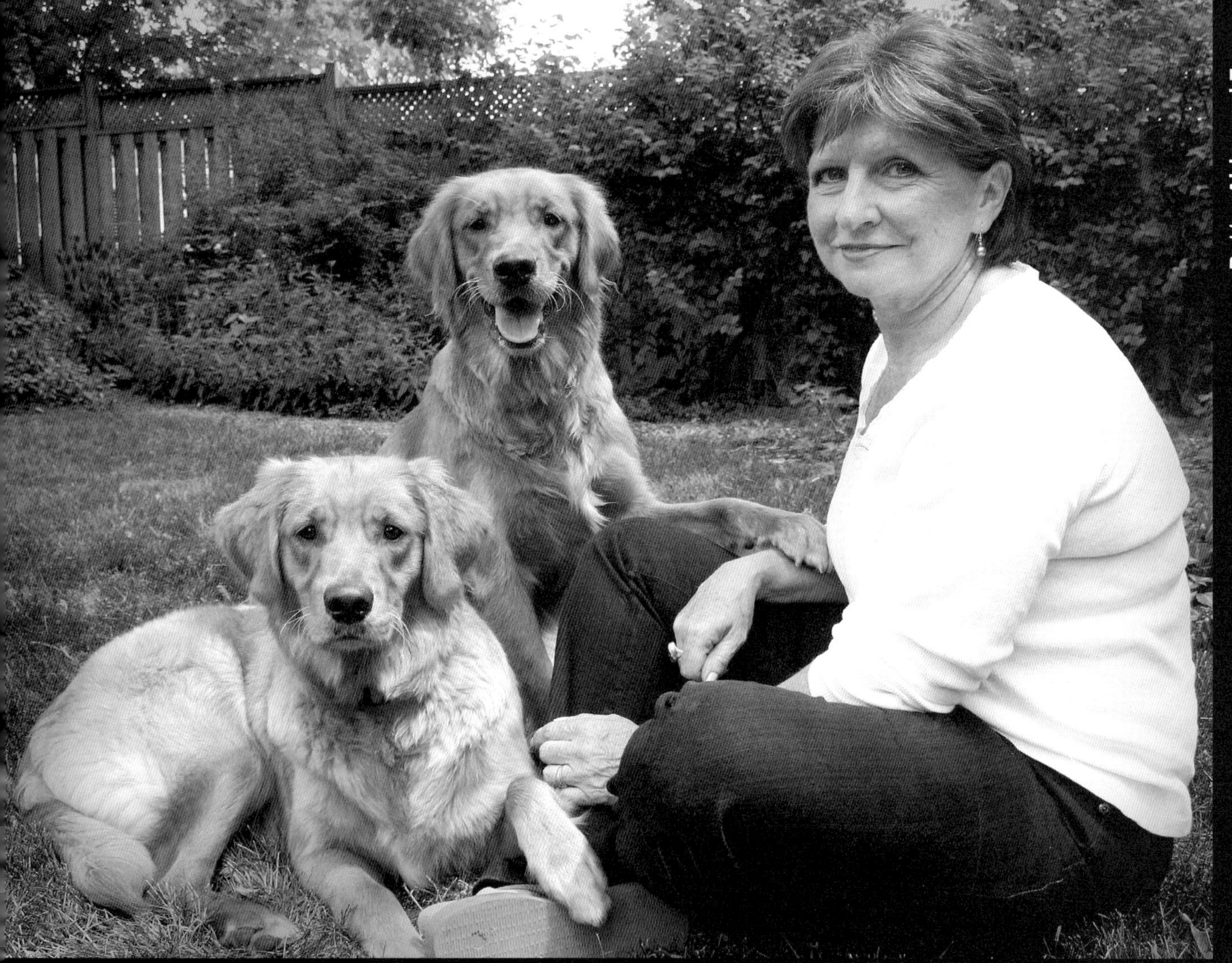


Their sweet and fun-loving personalities

make every day a Golden day.

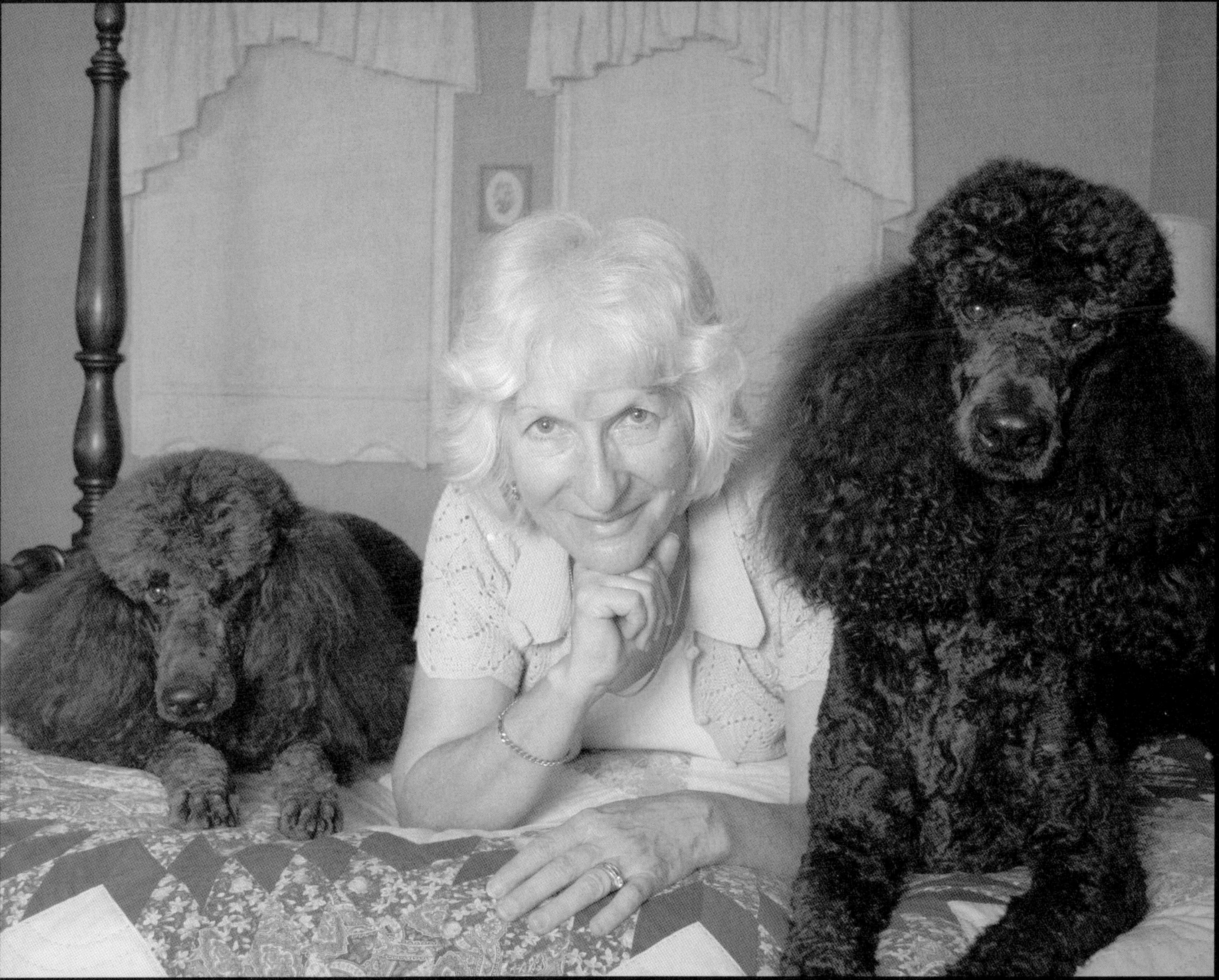

Chablis and Cosette don't mind sharing my bed

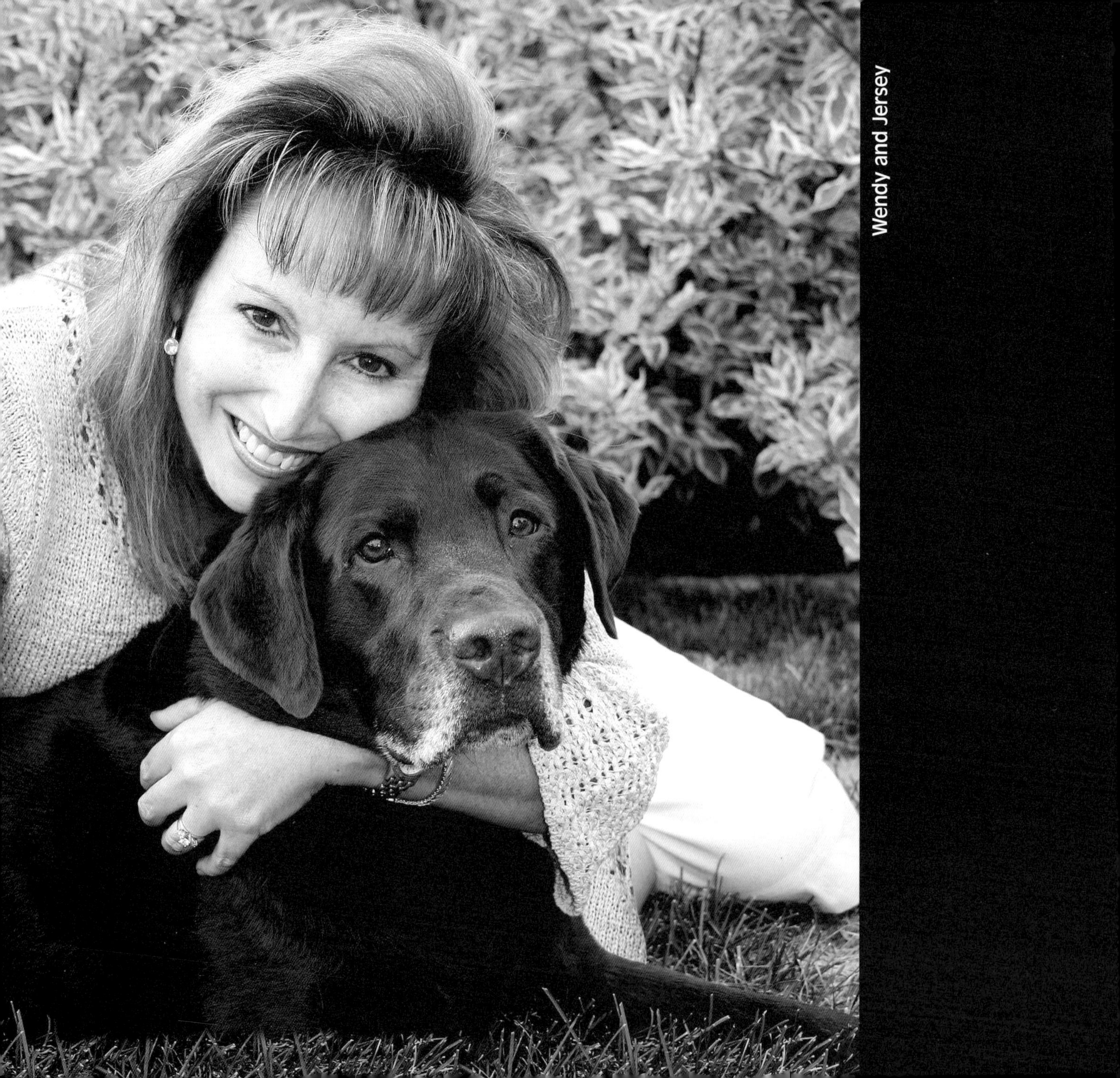
Wendy and Jersey

When I leave for work

every morning,

Jersey barks, pleading

with me to stay home

and play with him.

I wish life were so

simple.

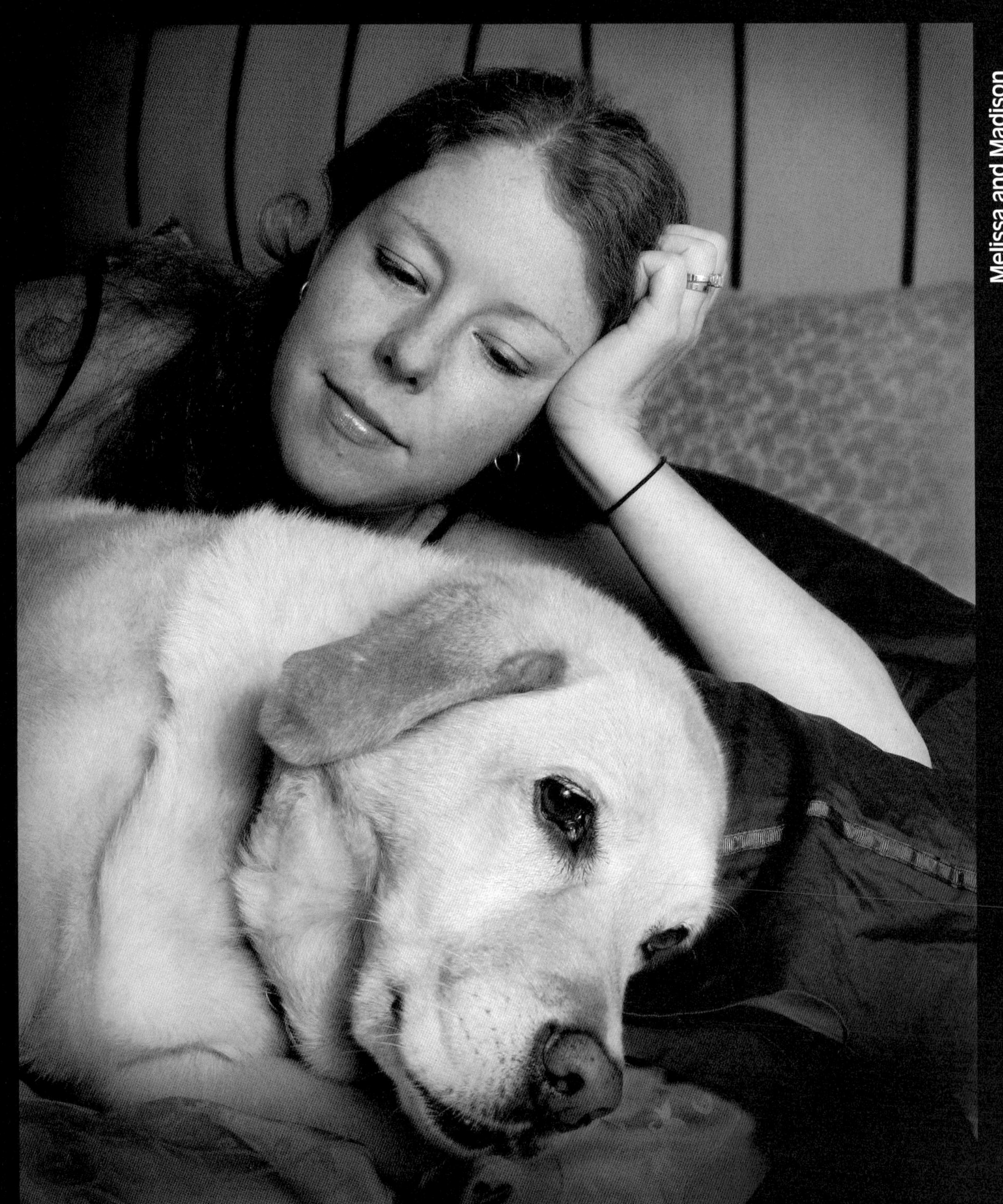

Melissa and Madison

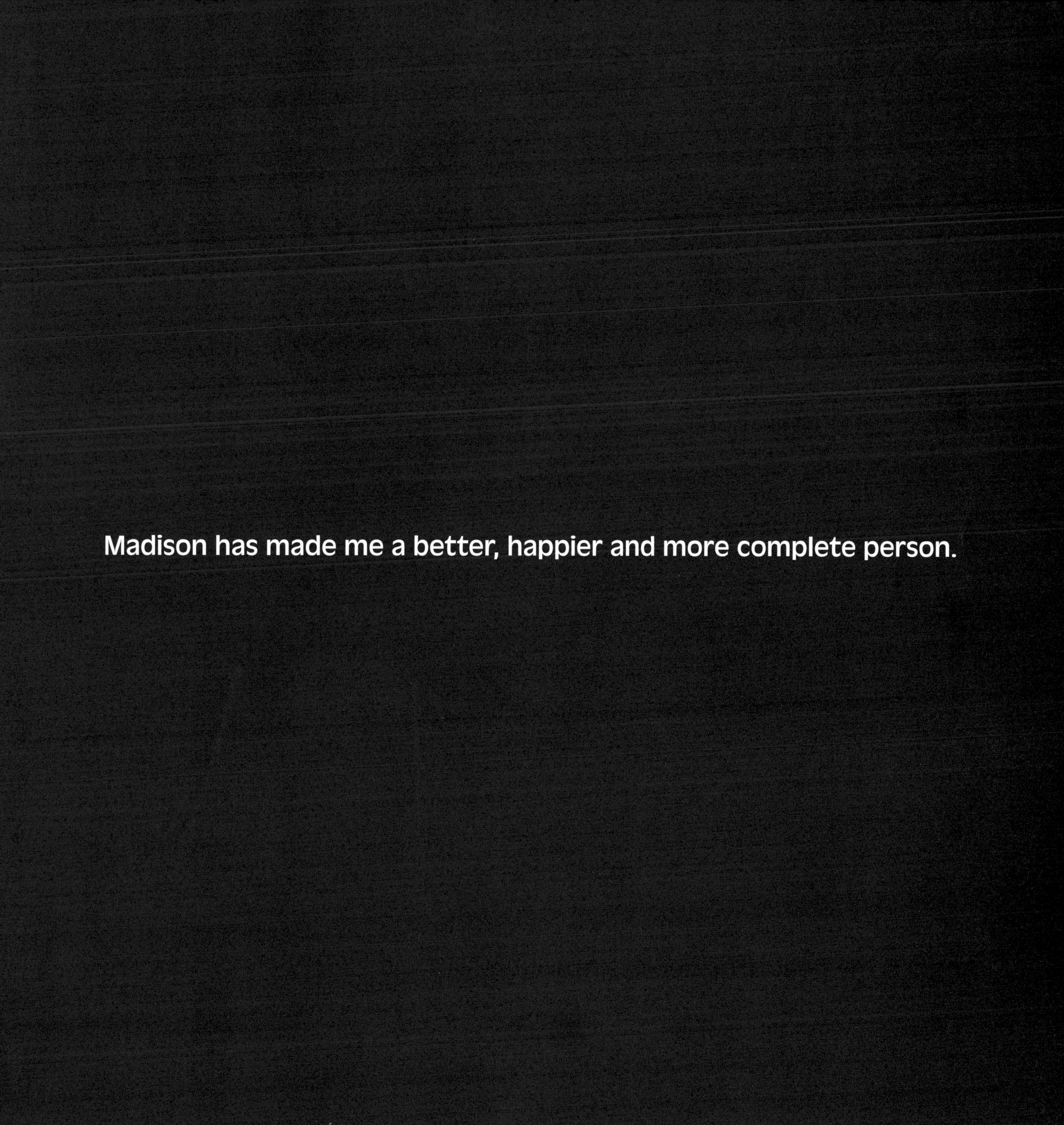
Madison has made me a better, happier and more complete person.

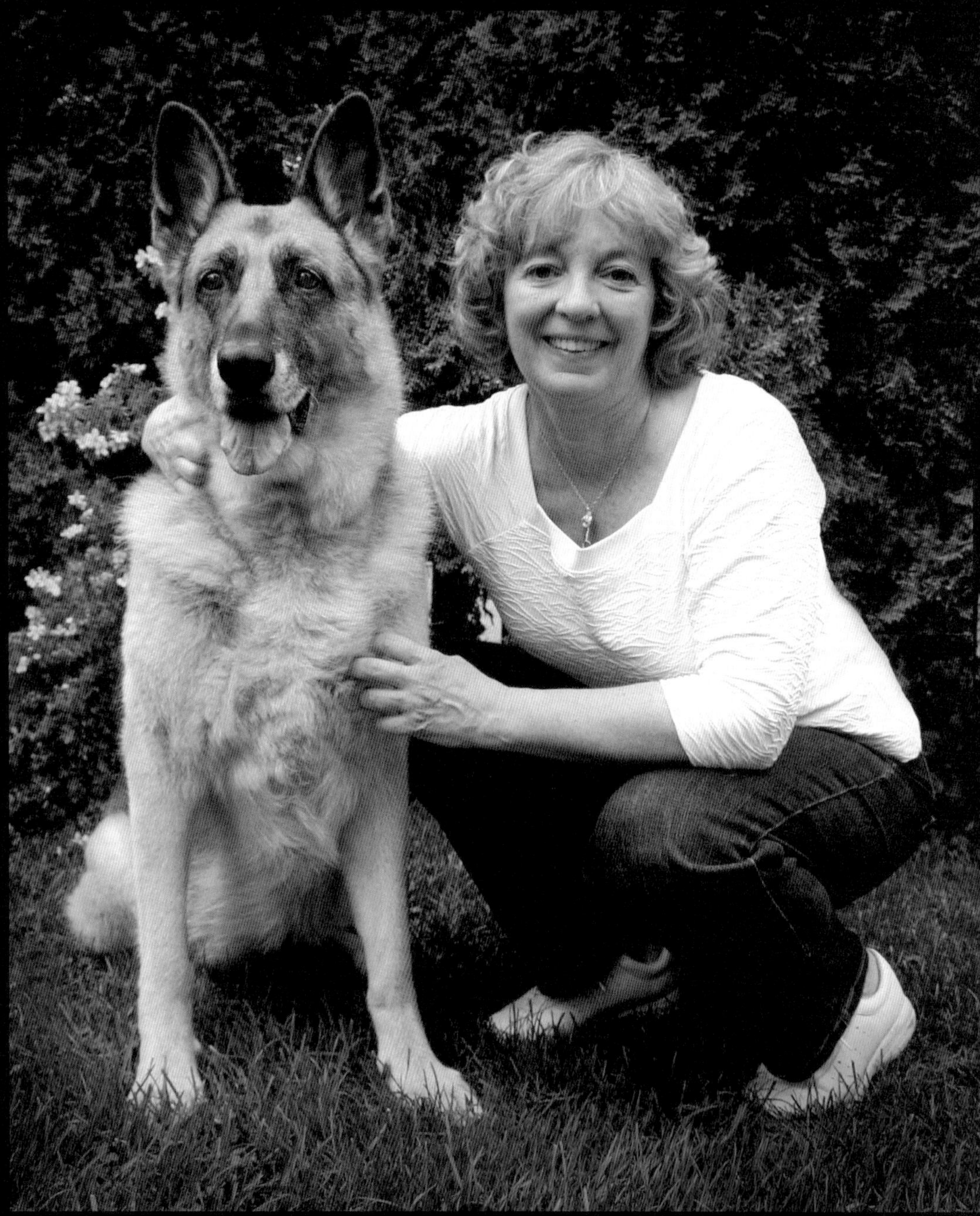



Angel is my beautiful, gentle, intelligent girl with a slightly crooked halo.

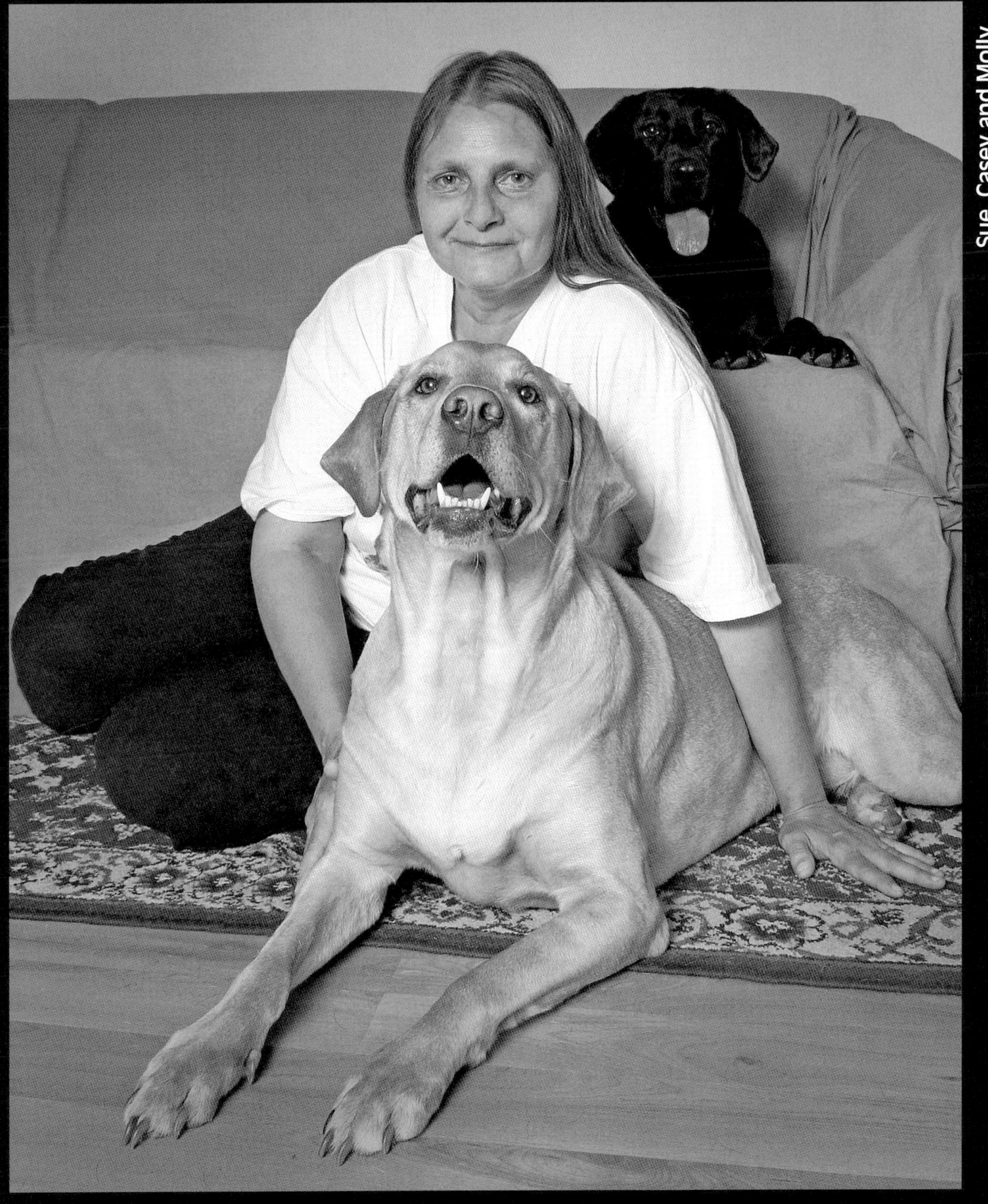


Casey and Molly came to stay with me 'temporarily.'

Years later, they are still here and none of us have any plans to go elsewhere.

I  rescued my dogs,

but the truth is that they rescued me.

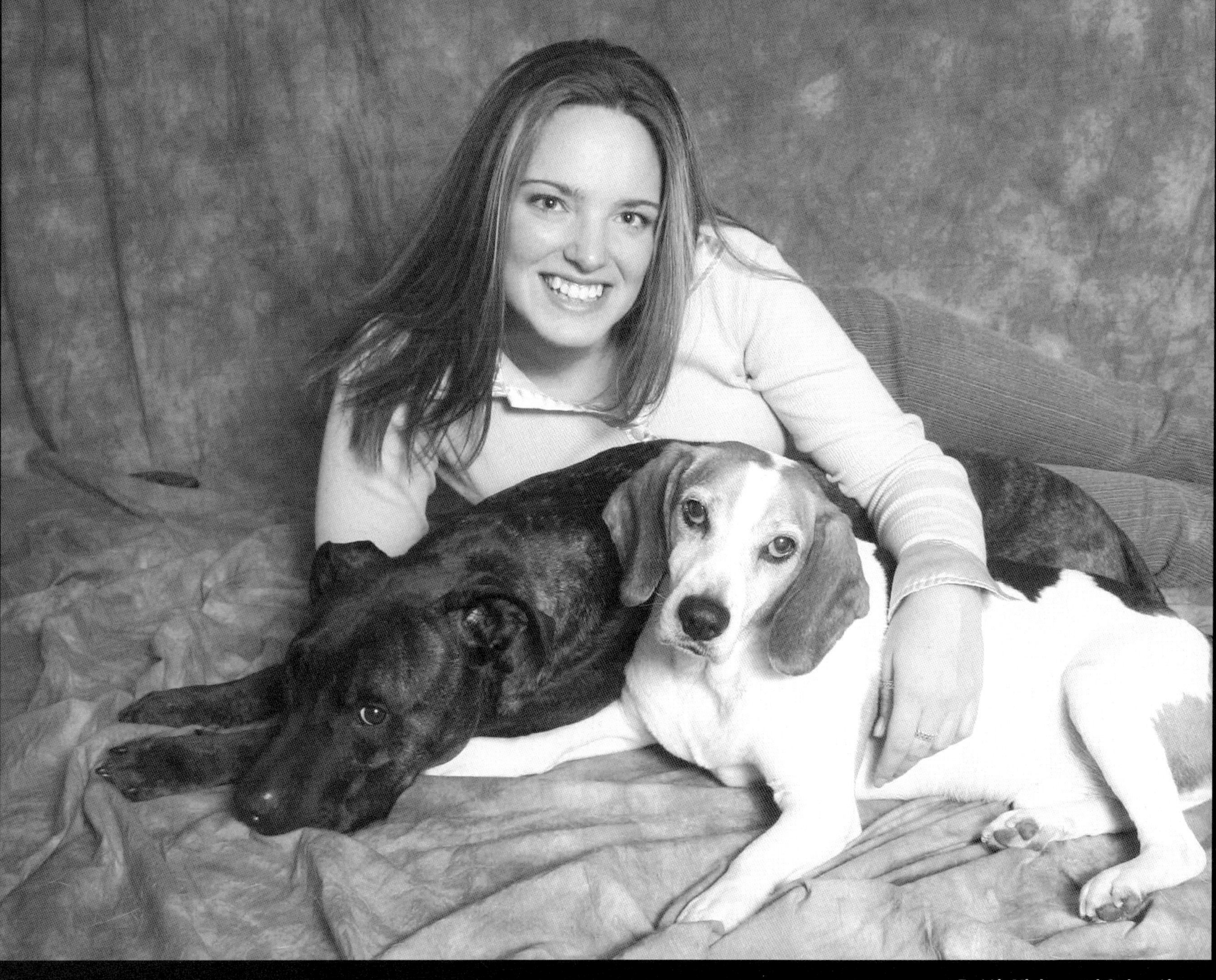

Patti, Nicky and Sebastian

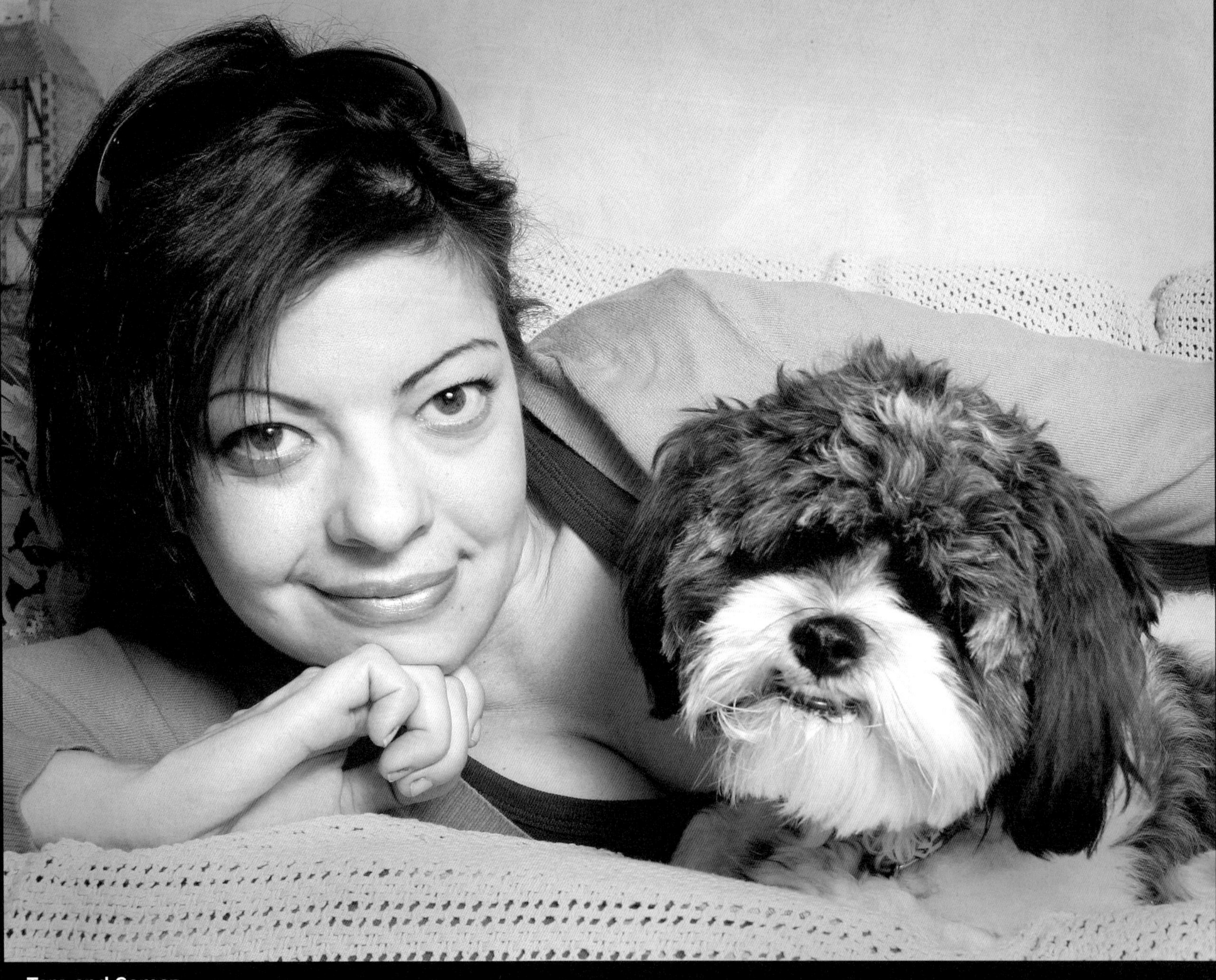

Tara and Gomez

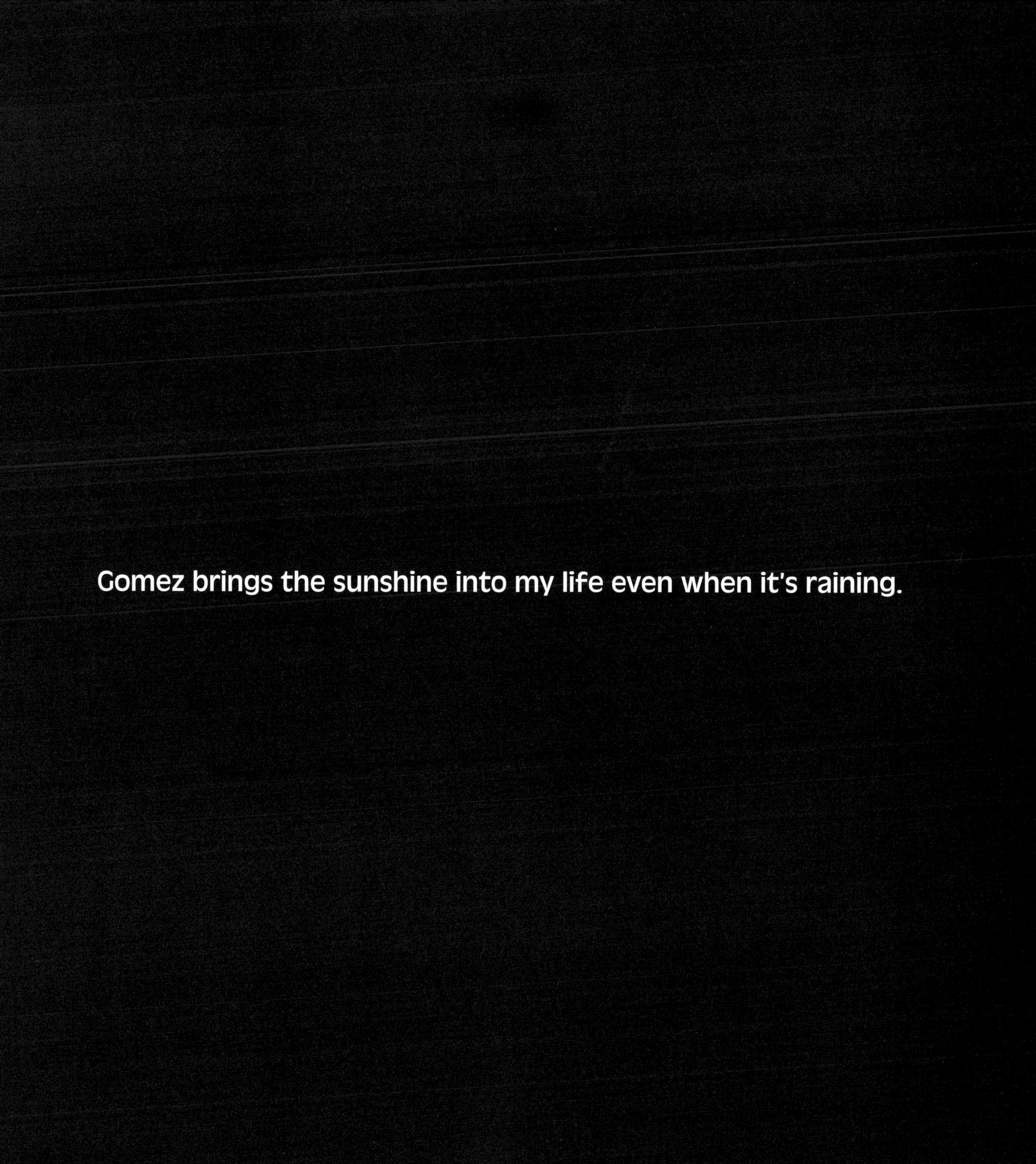
Gomez brings the sunshine into my life even when it's raining.

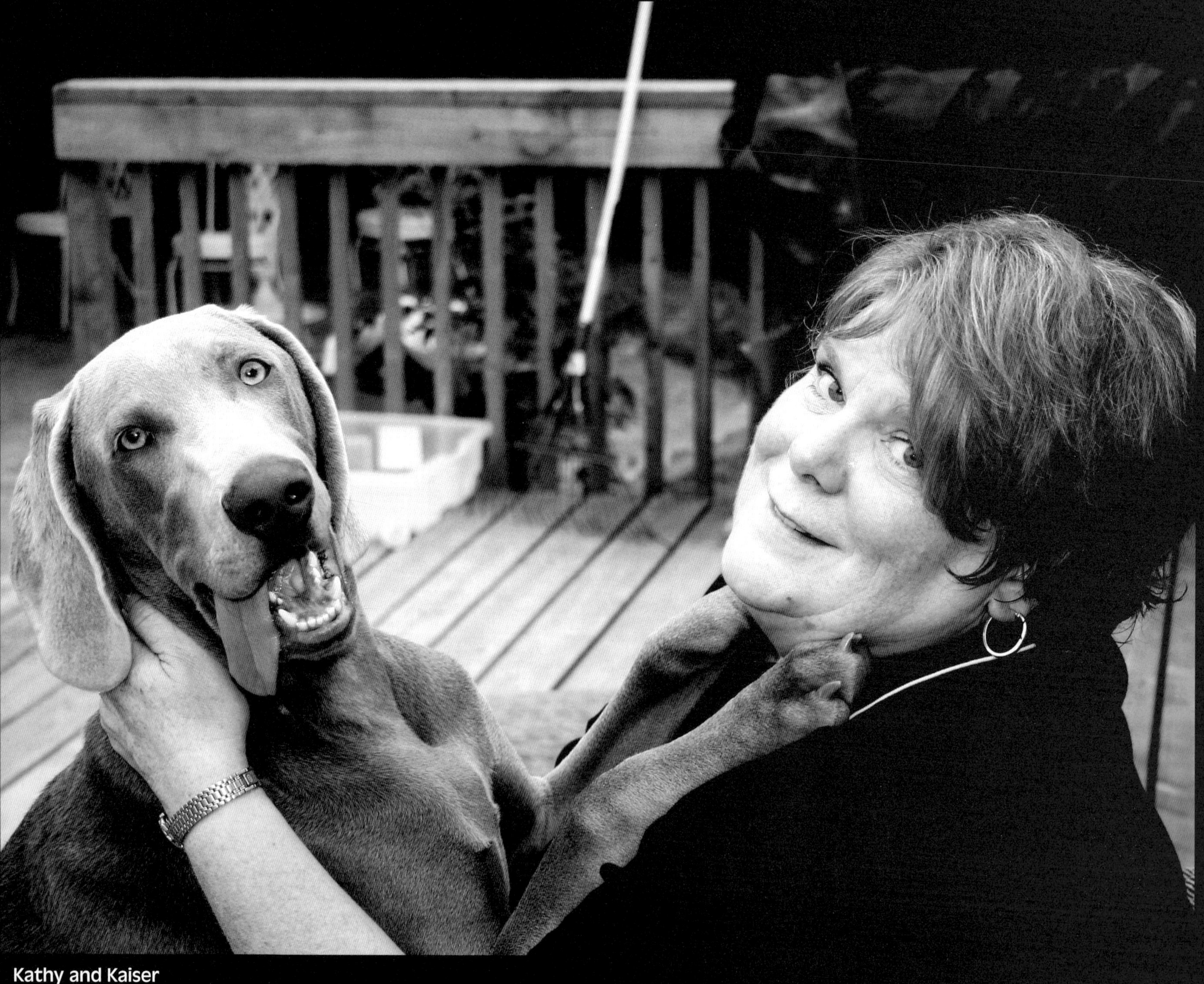

Kathy and Kaiser

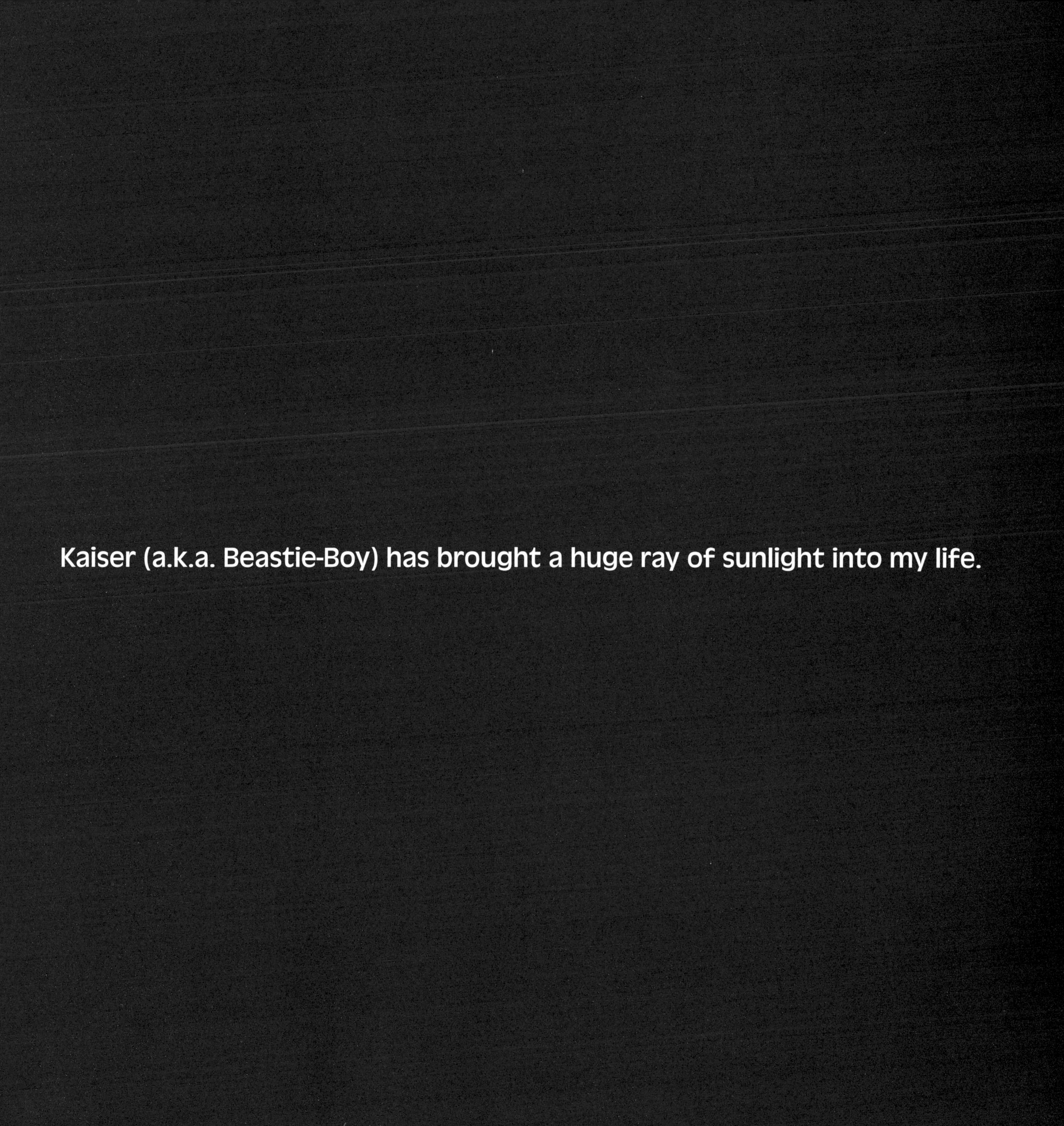

Kaiser (a.k.a. Beastie-Boy) has brought a huge ray of sunlight into my life.

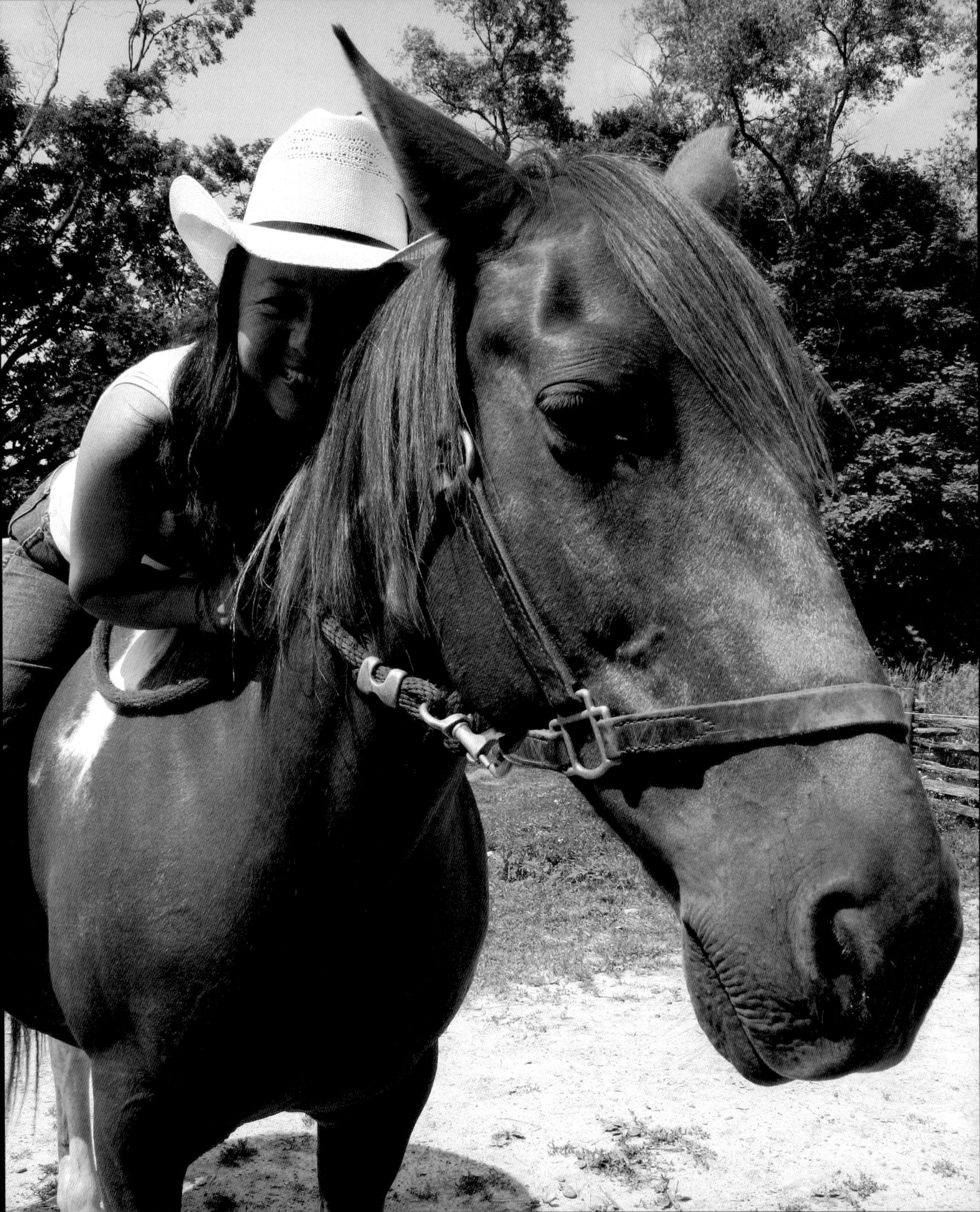

Oylian and Toes

Toes threw me a few times,

stepped on my foot and broke my toe - twice.

I had always wondered why her previous owner changed her

name from Bella to Toes.

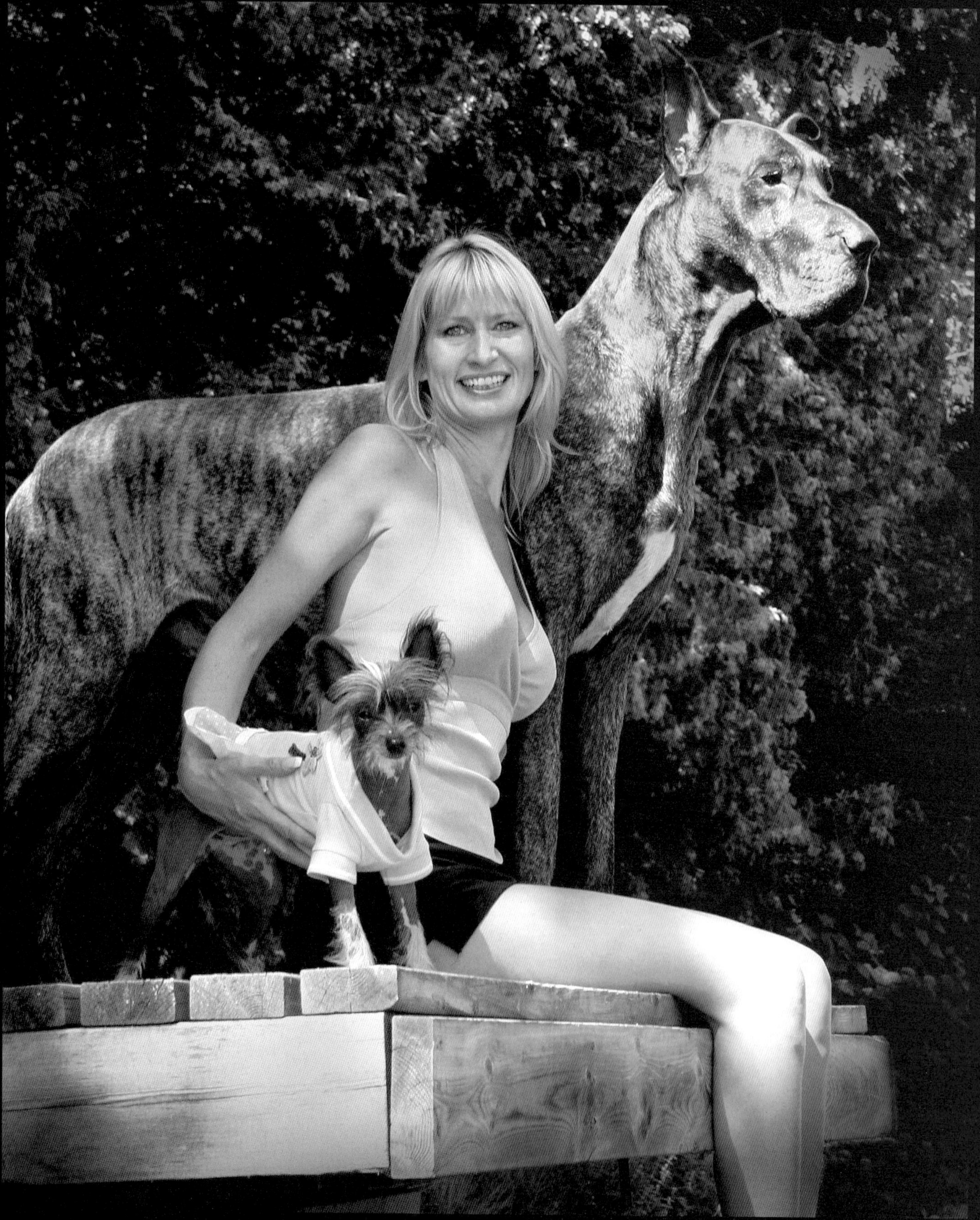

Kim, Colton and BlueBell

My dogs are my family,

my passion,

my addiction,

my anti-depressant.

Our dogs may be completely different in appearance

but they are soulmates just the same.

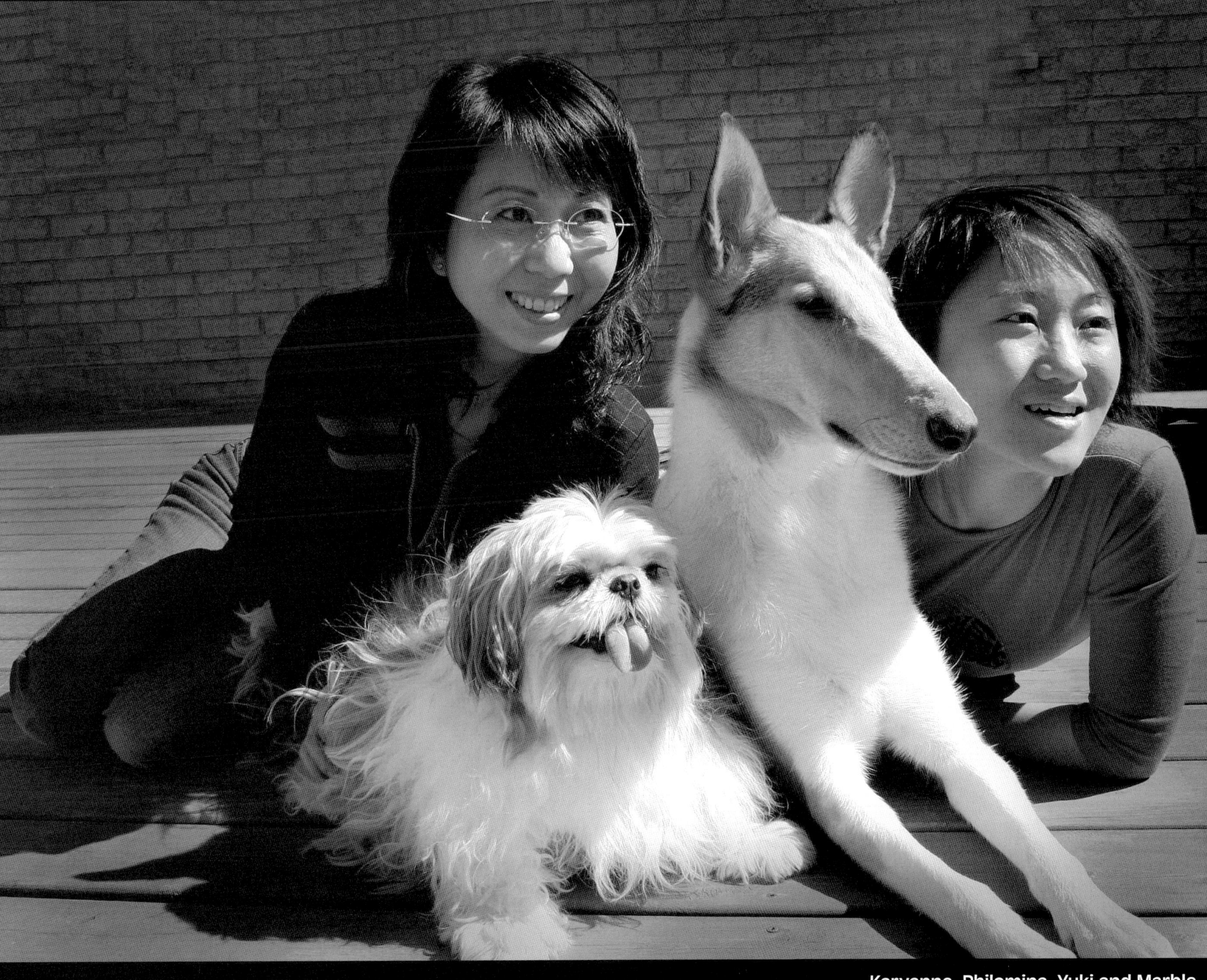

Karyanne, Philomina, Yuki and Marble

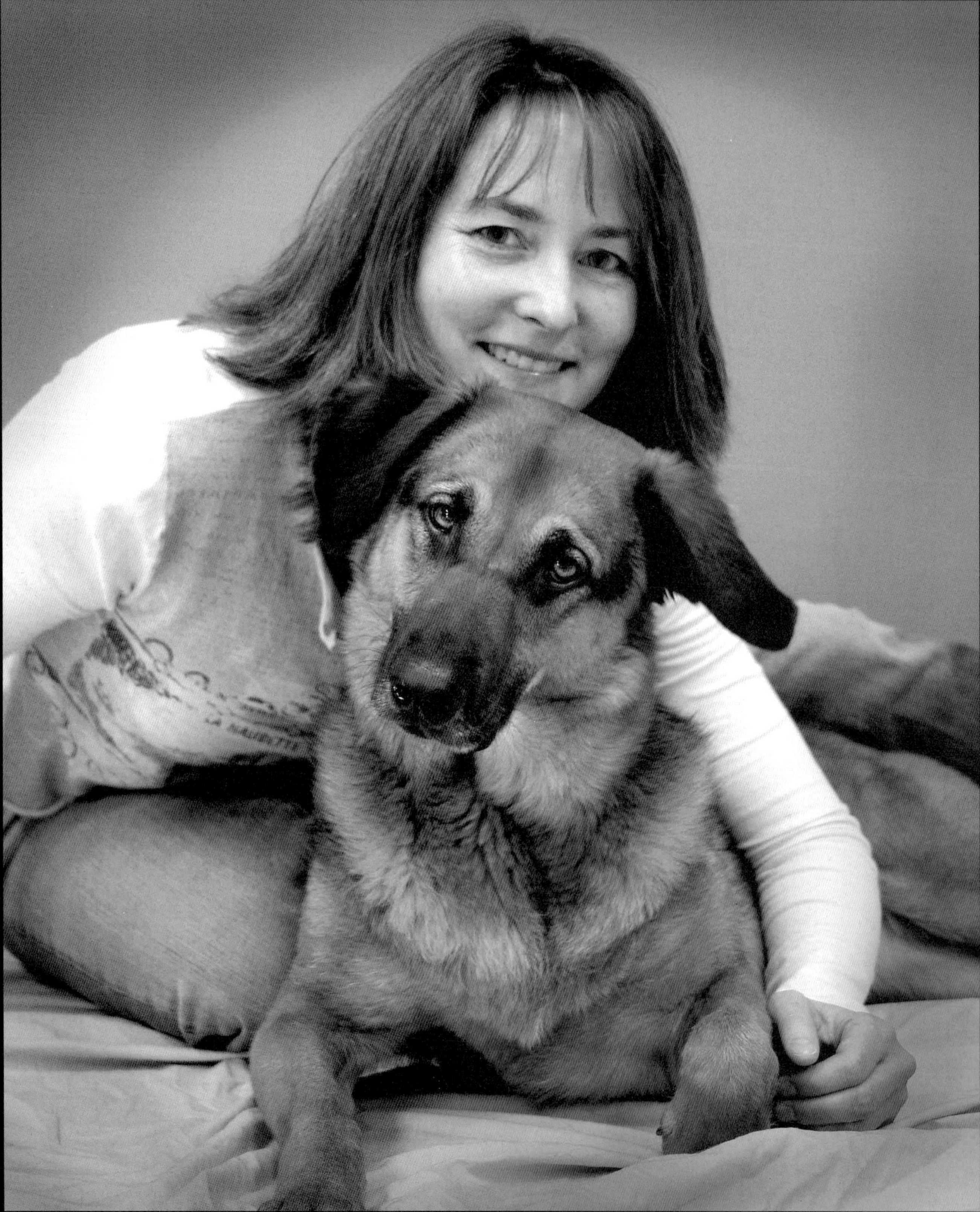

Cheryl and Abby

I can watch her for hours,

even if she is doing absolutely nothing.

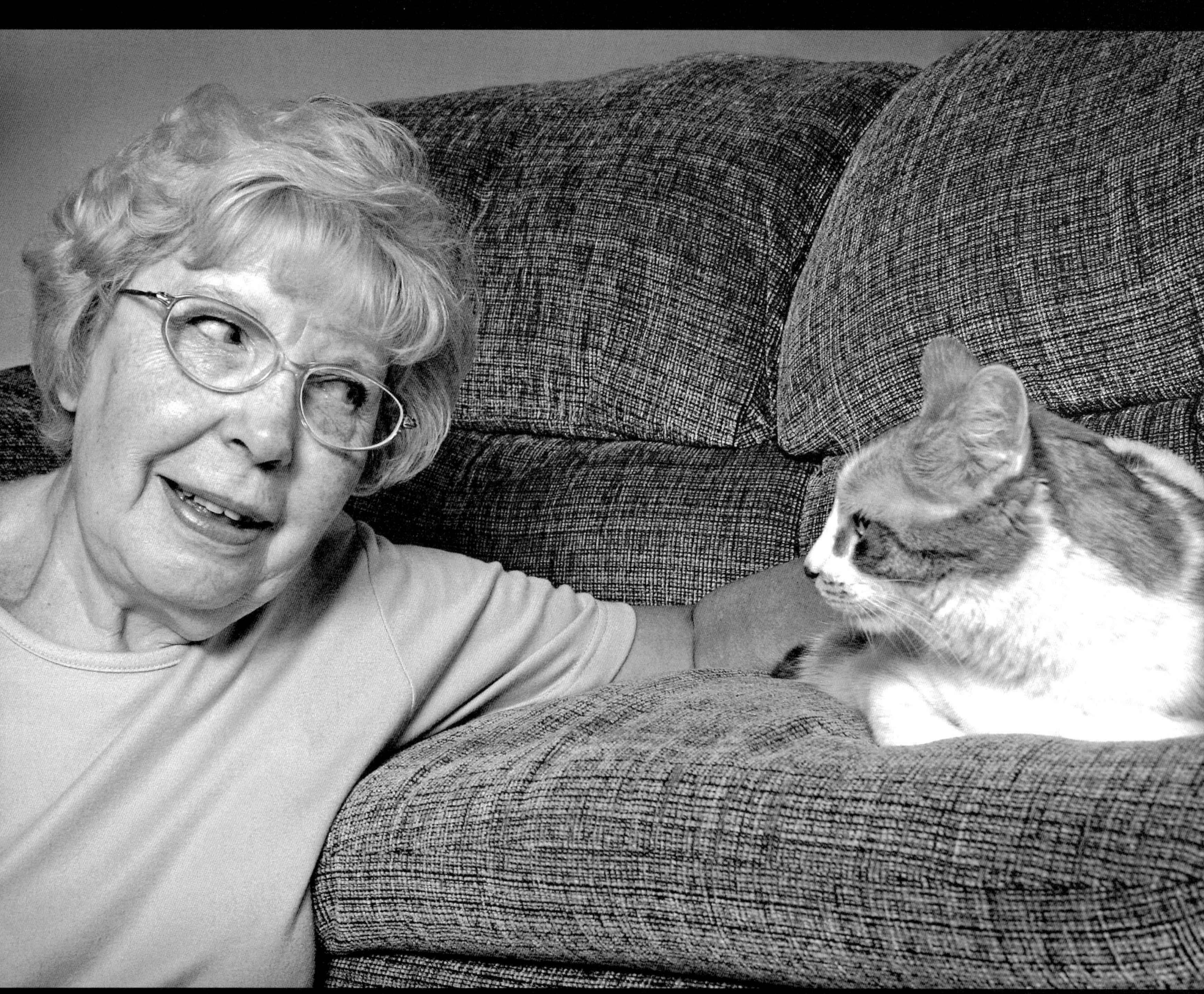


Is there anything wrong with this picture?
Eileen and Byron

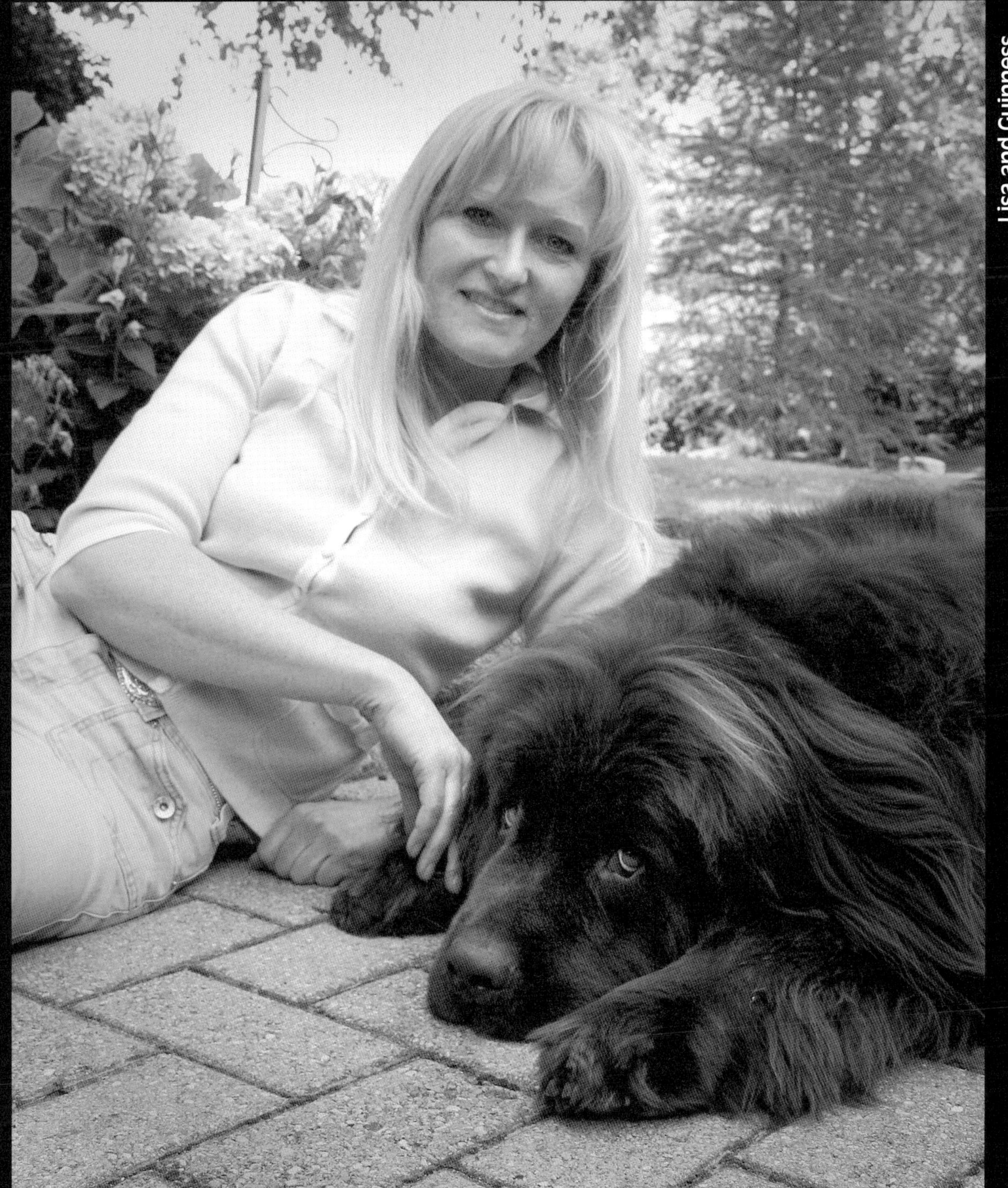



My dog and I are the best of friends

and we love each other unconditionally.

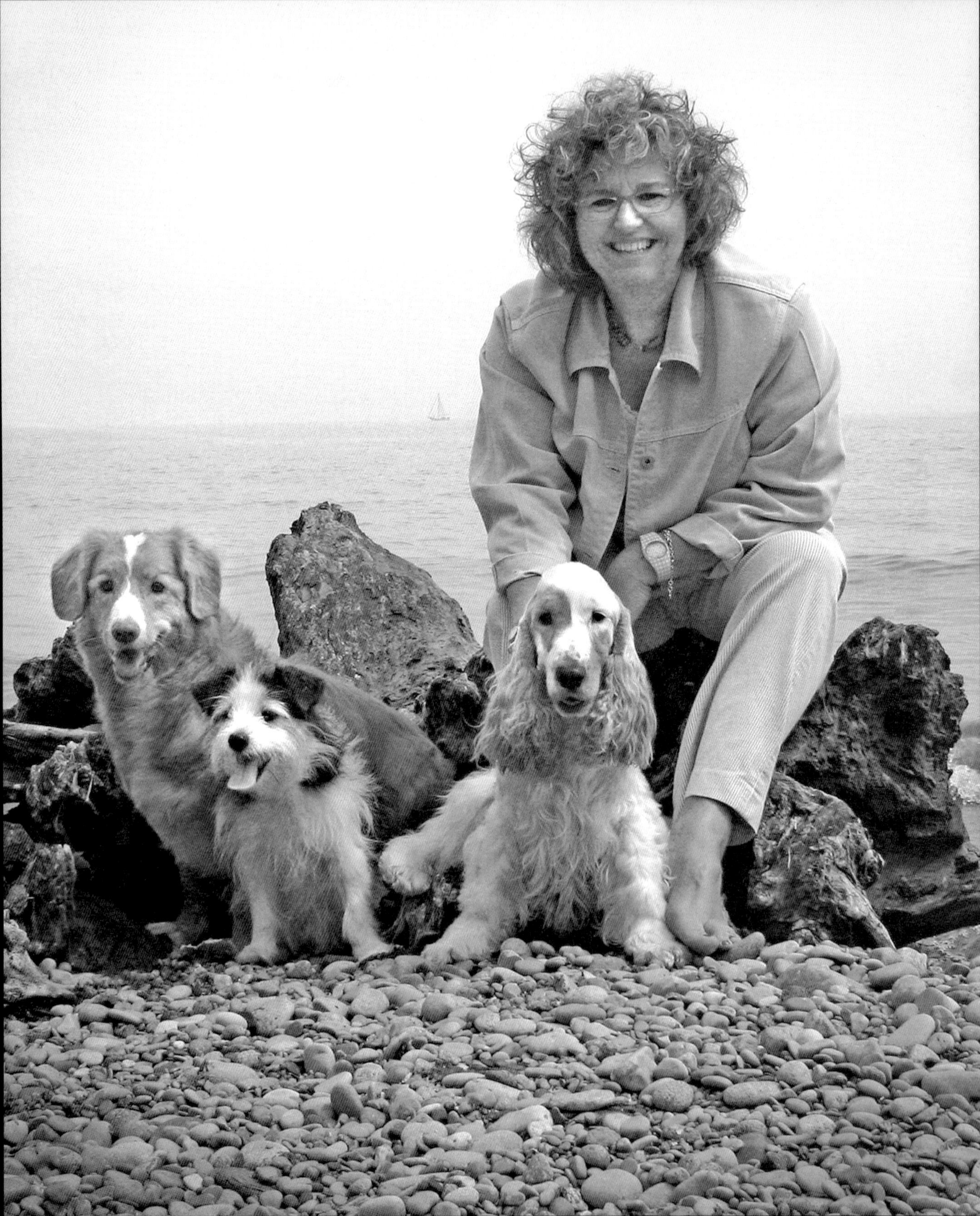

Gillian, Cruiser, Levi and Yardley

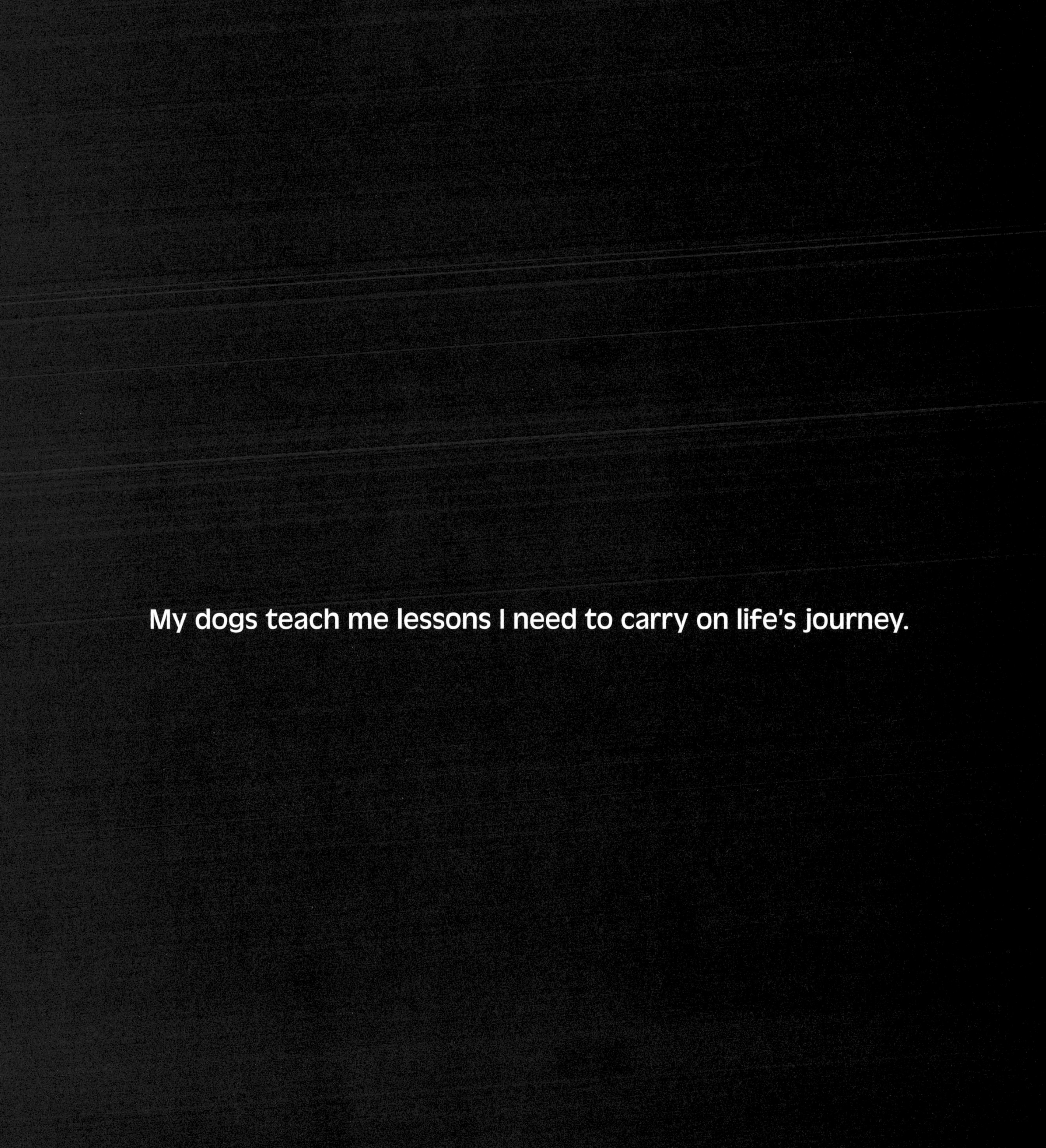
My dogs teach me lessons I need to carry on life's journey.

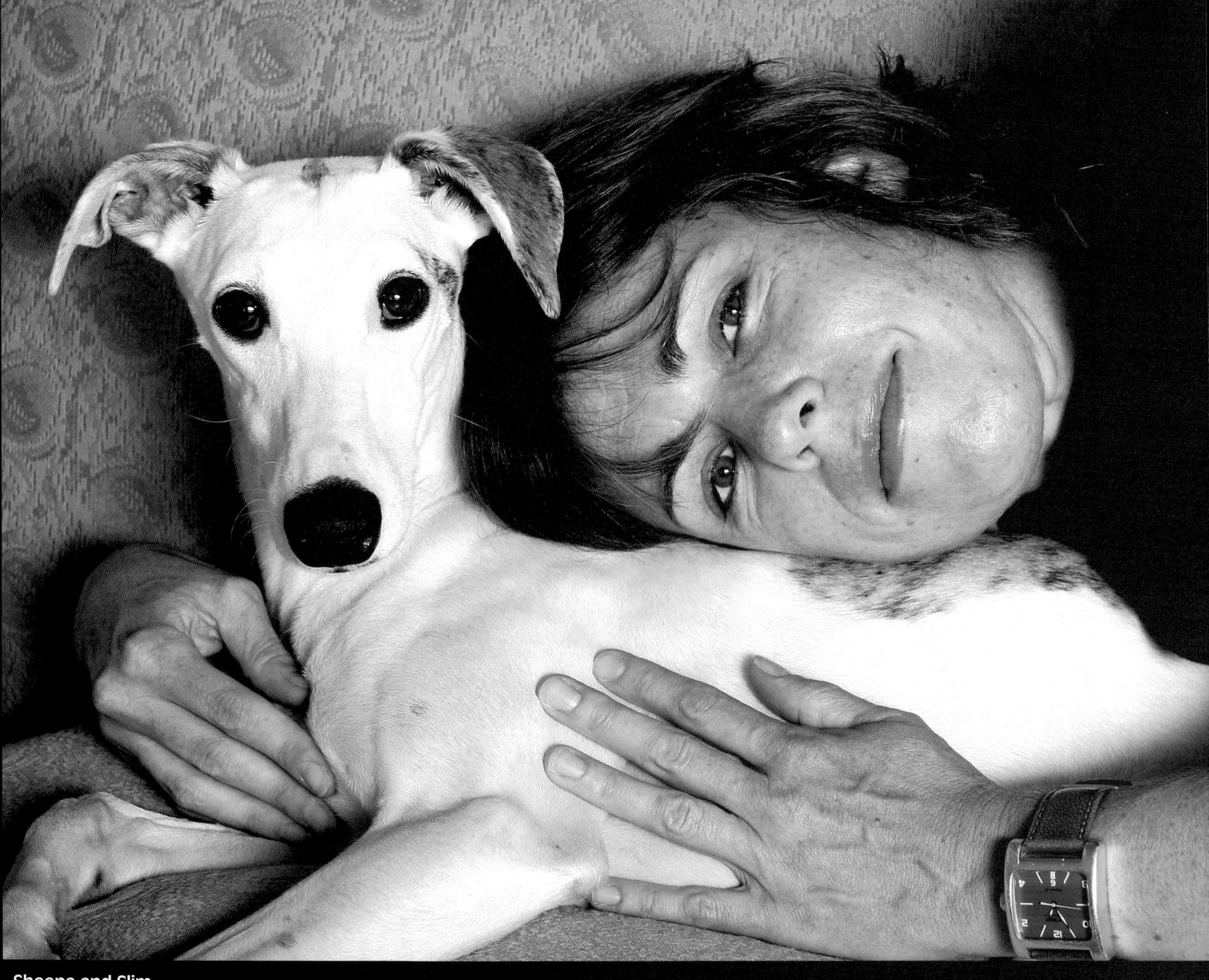

Sheena and Slim

He can spring six feet into the air

when I'm preparing his dinner,

yet won't move a muscle

when it's time to get out of bed.

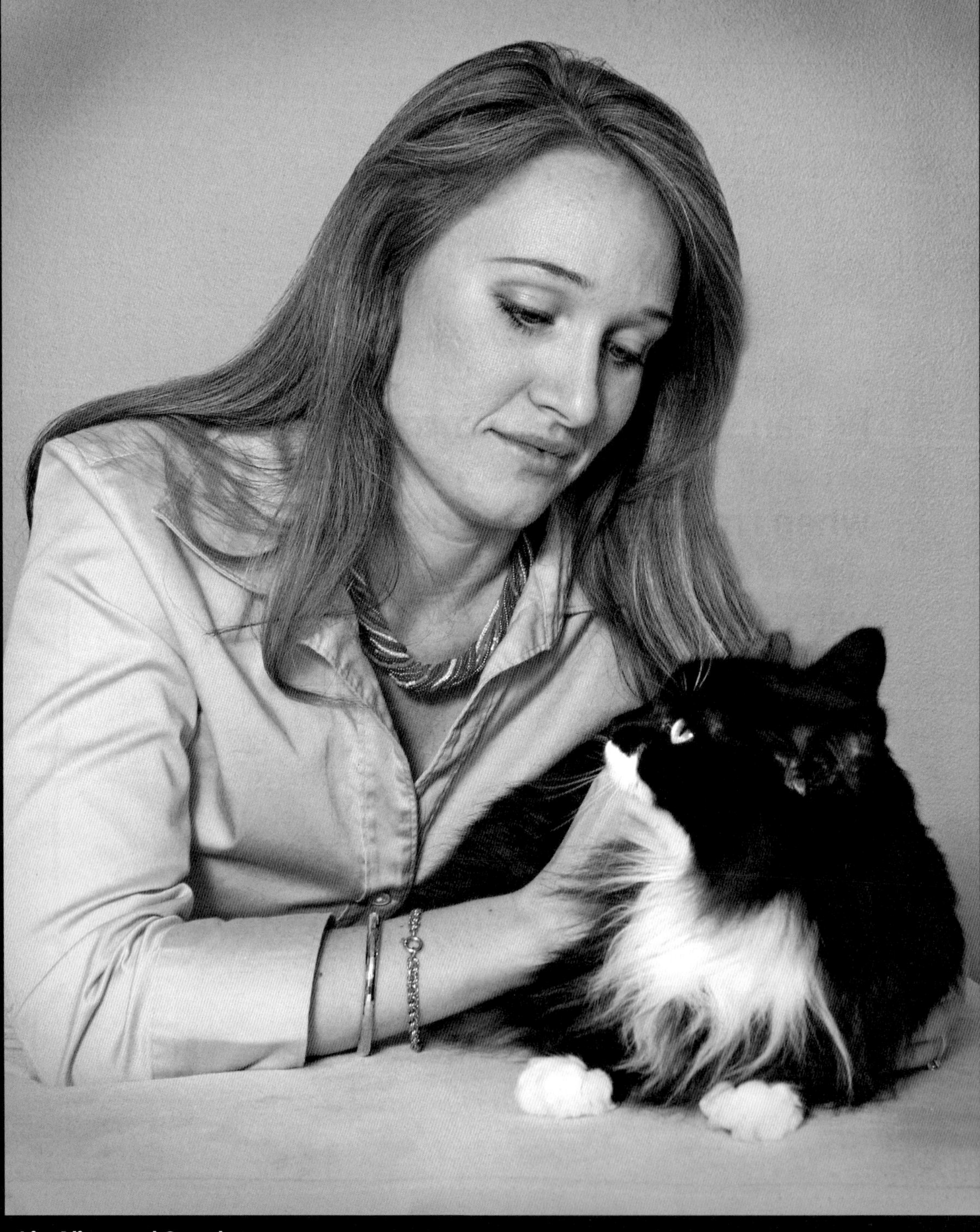

**Liv-Aline and Spooky**

If there's any truth to the theory that stress-free

living increases longevity,

Spooky will live to 50.

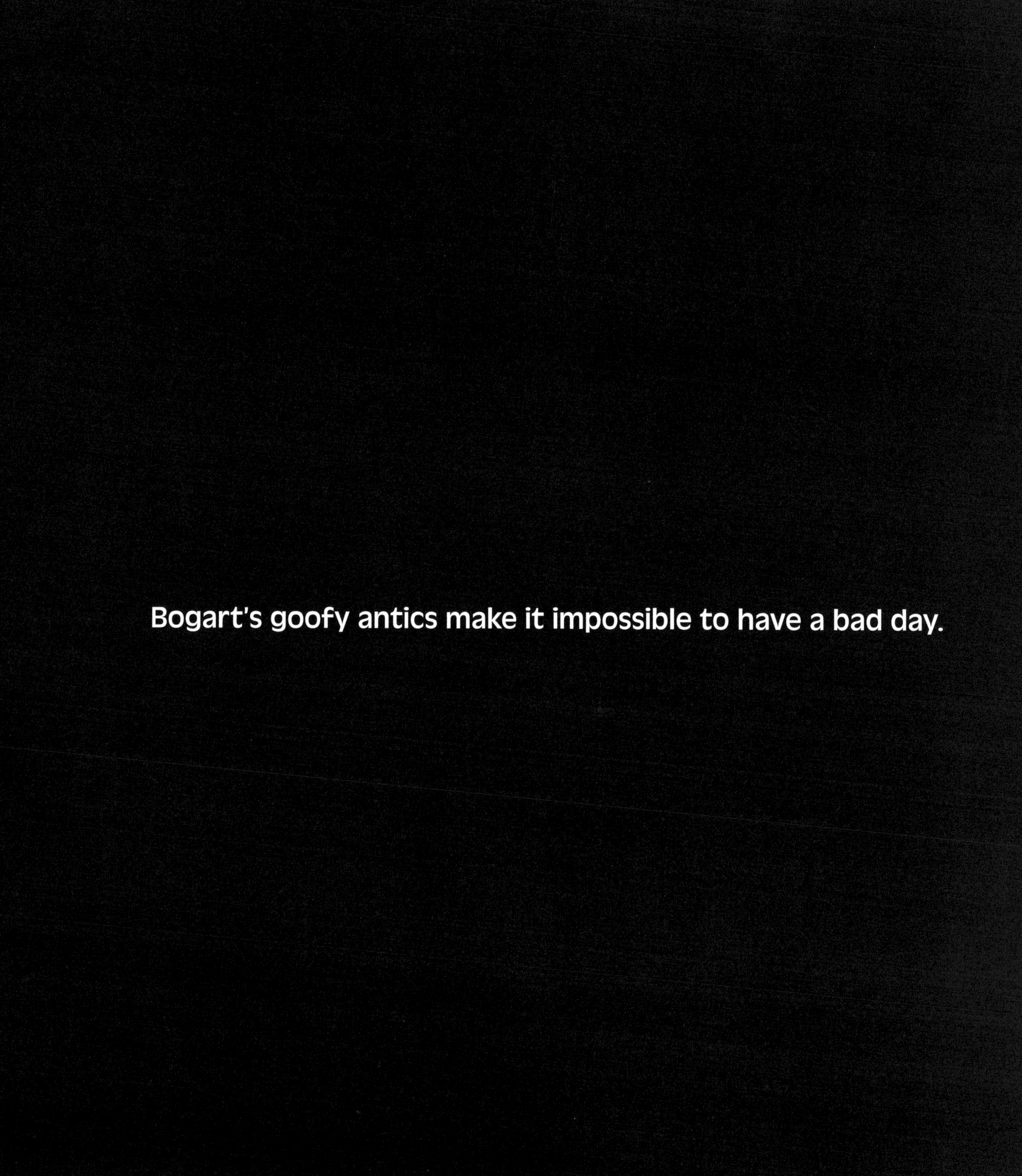

Bogart's goofy antics make it impossible to have a bad day.

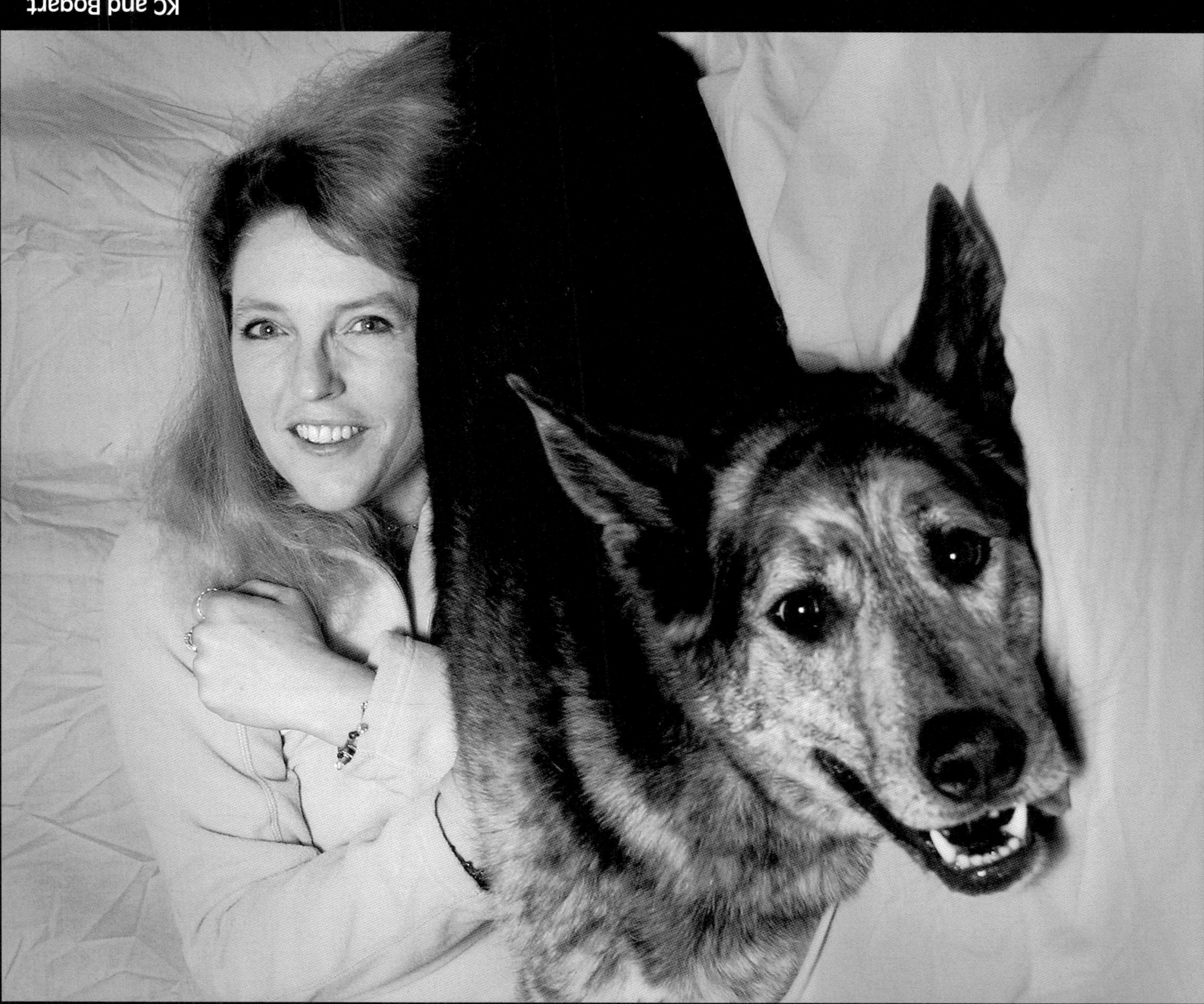
KC and Bogart

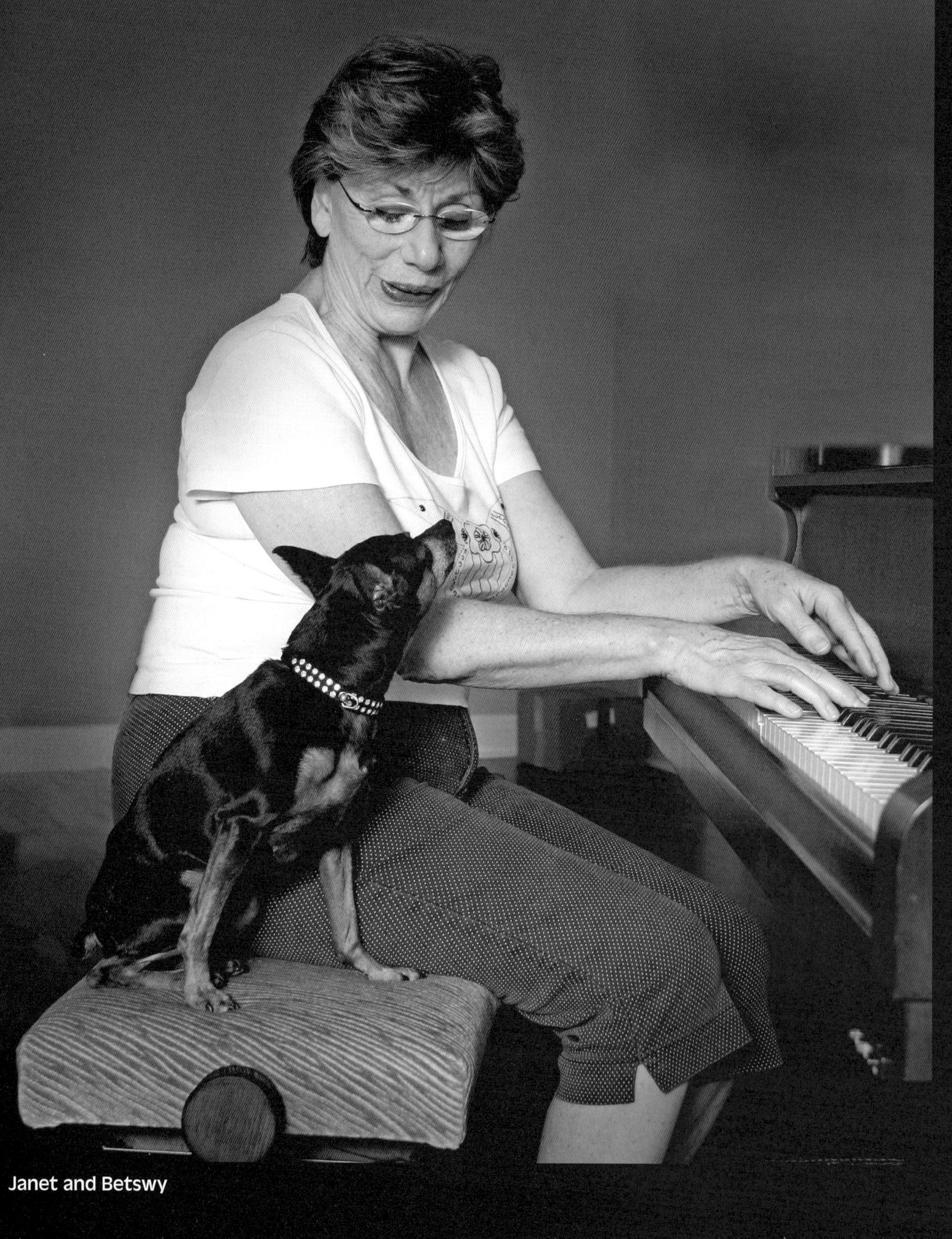



Janet and Betswy

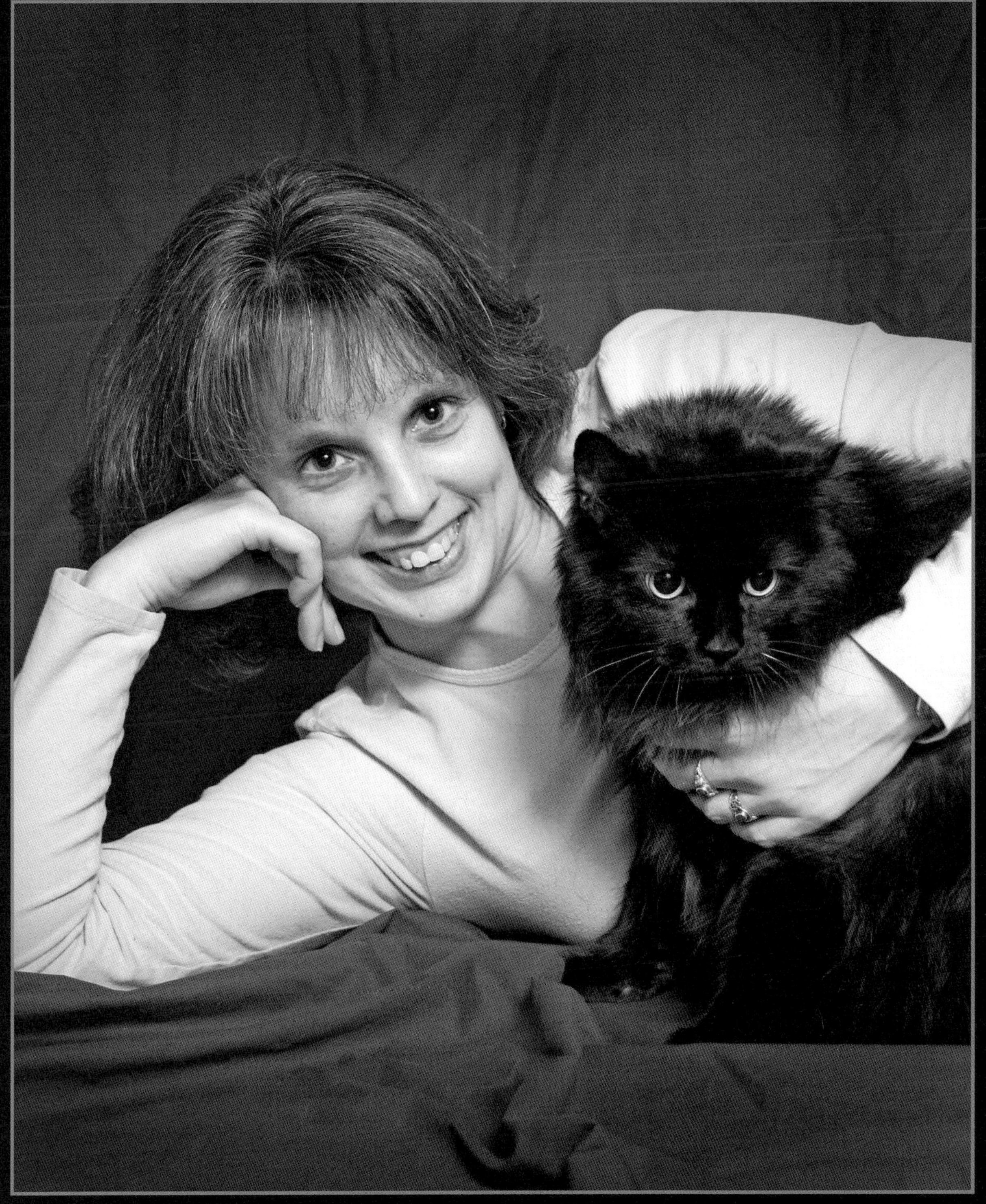


Bear will sit, listen and help me de-stress after a hard day at work

I always thought my kids were the ultimate charmers,

but they are amateurs compared to these two dogs.

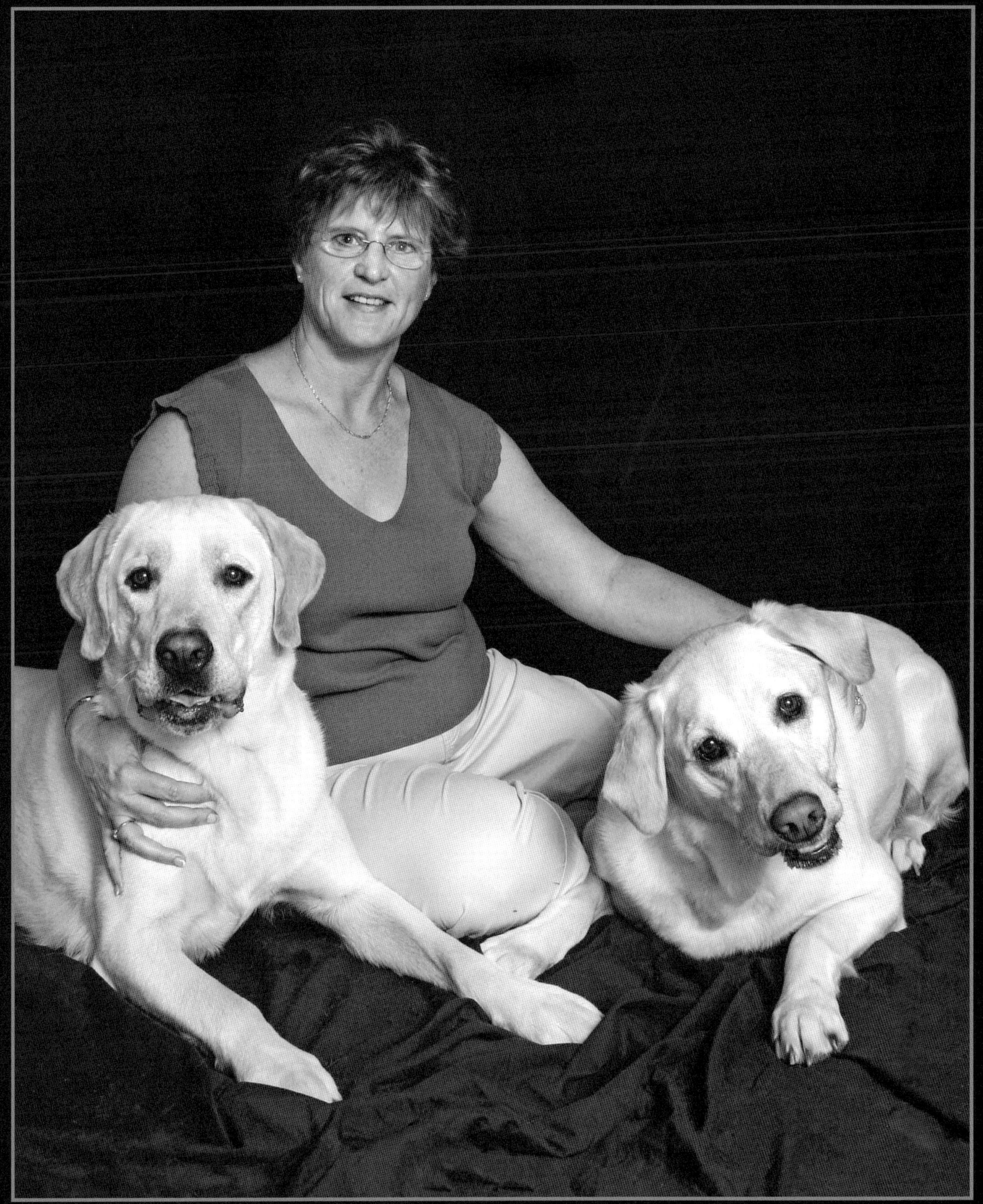

Kim, Toby and Callie

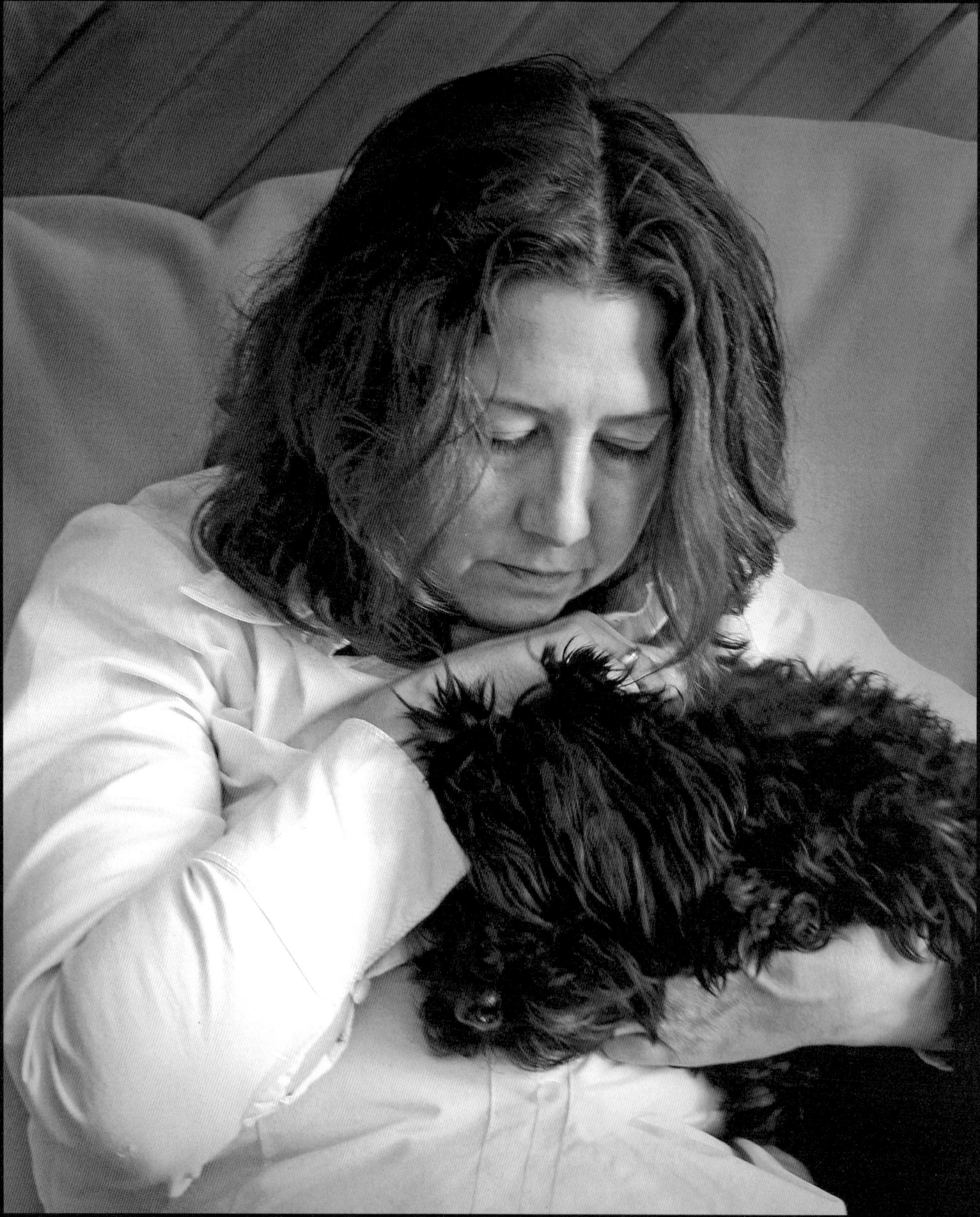

Lori and Keisha

She insists on taking her teddy bear

- and me -

with her to bed every night.

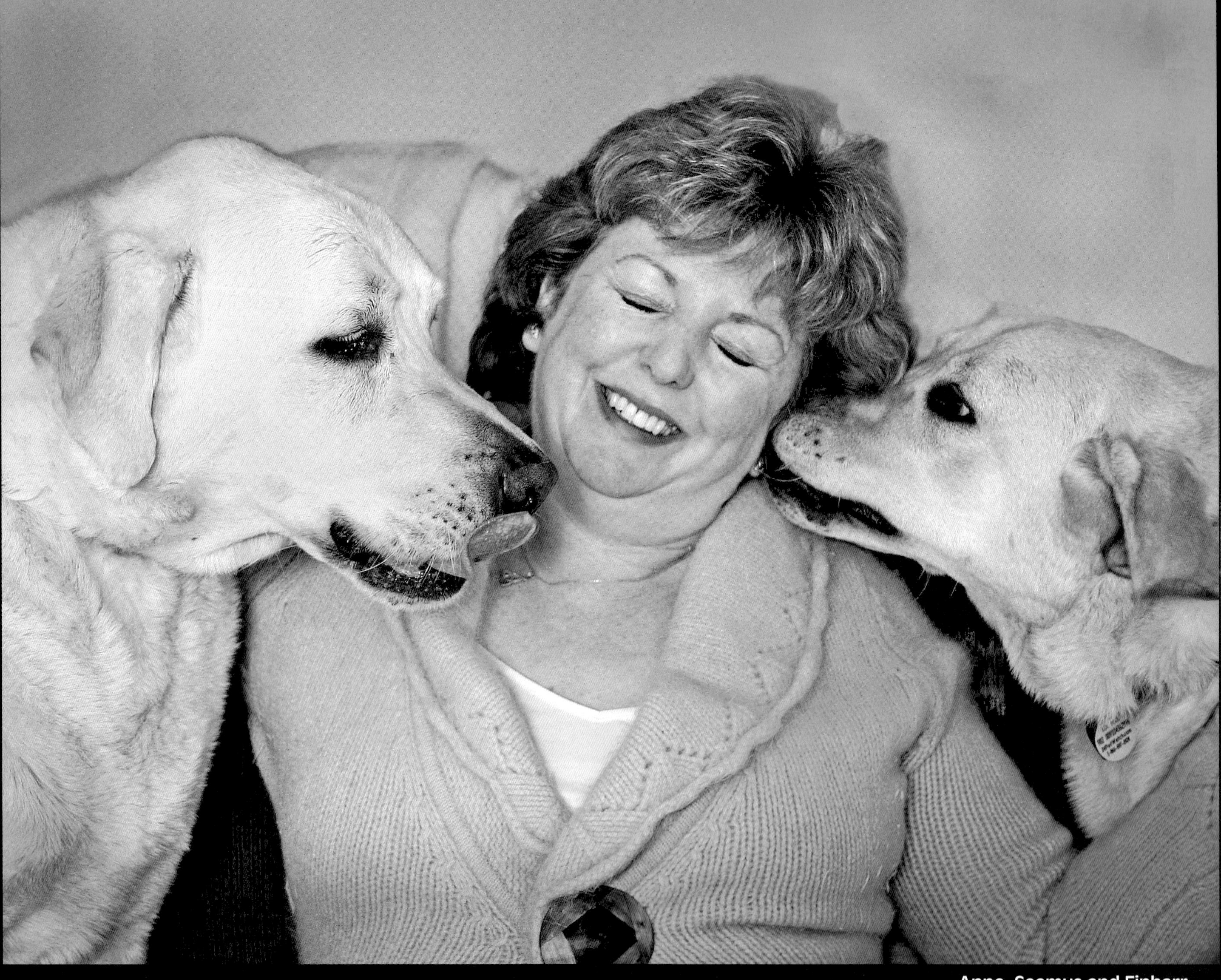

Anne, Seamus and Finbarr

My handsome boys wormed their way into my heart

with the same efficiency as they remove my makeup.

Fergus is a positive distraction,

always happy and good-natured.

I can't imagine my life without him.

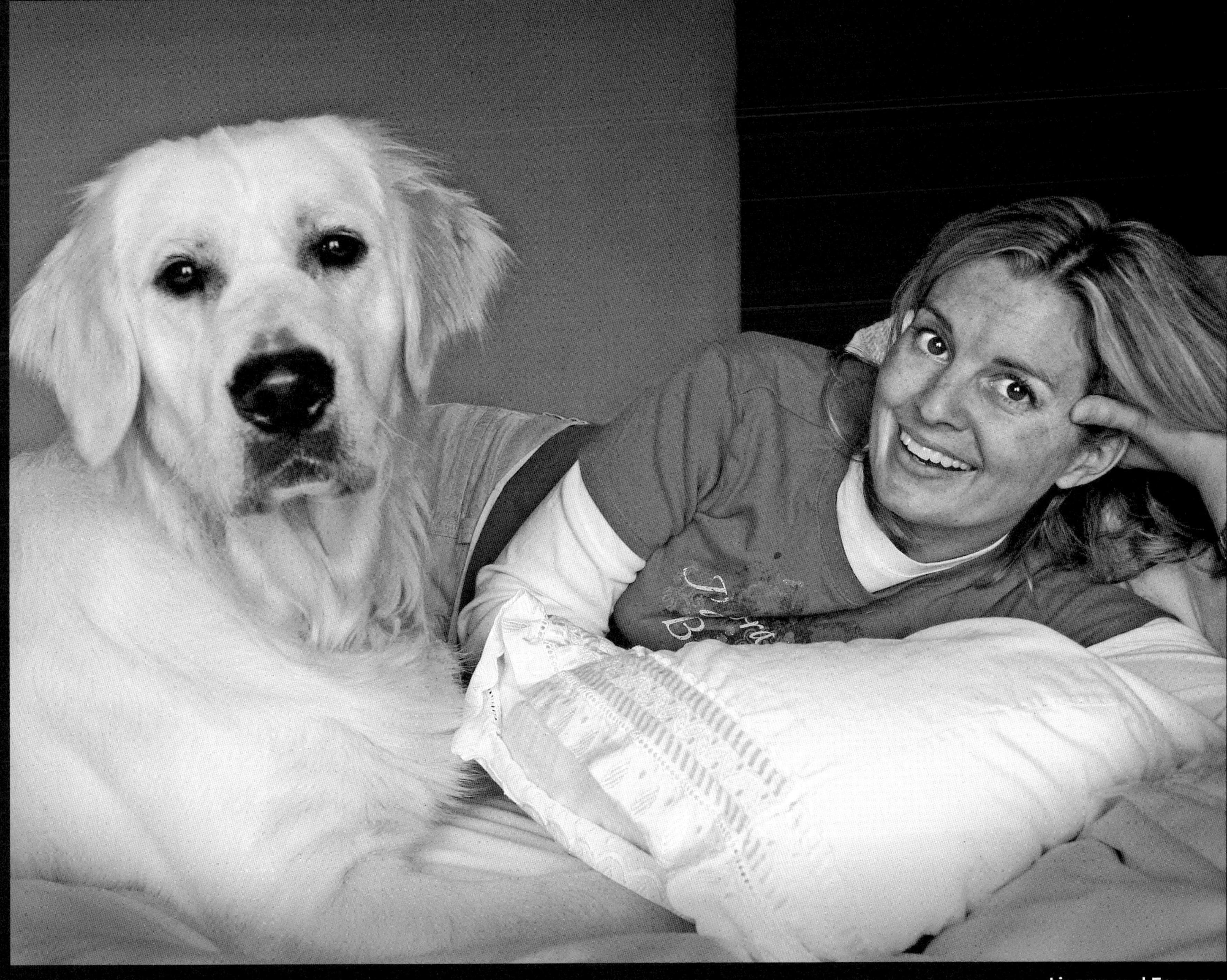

Lianne and Fergus

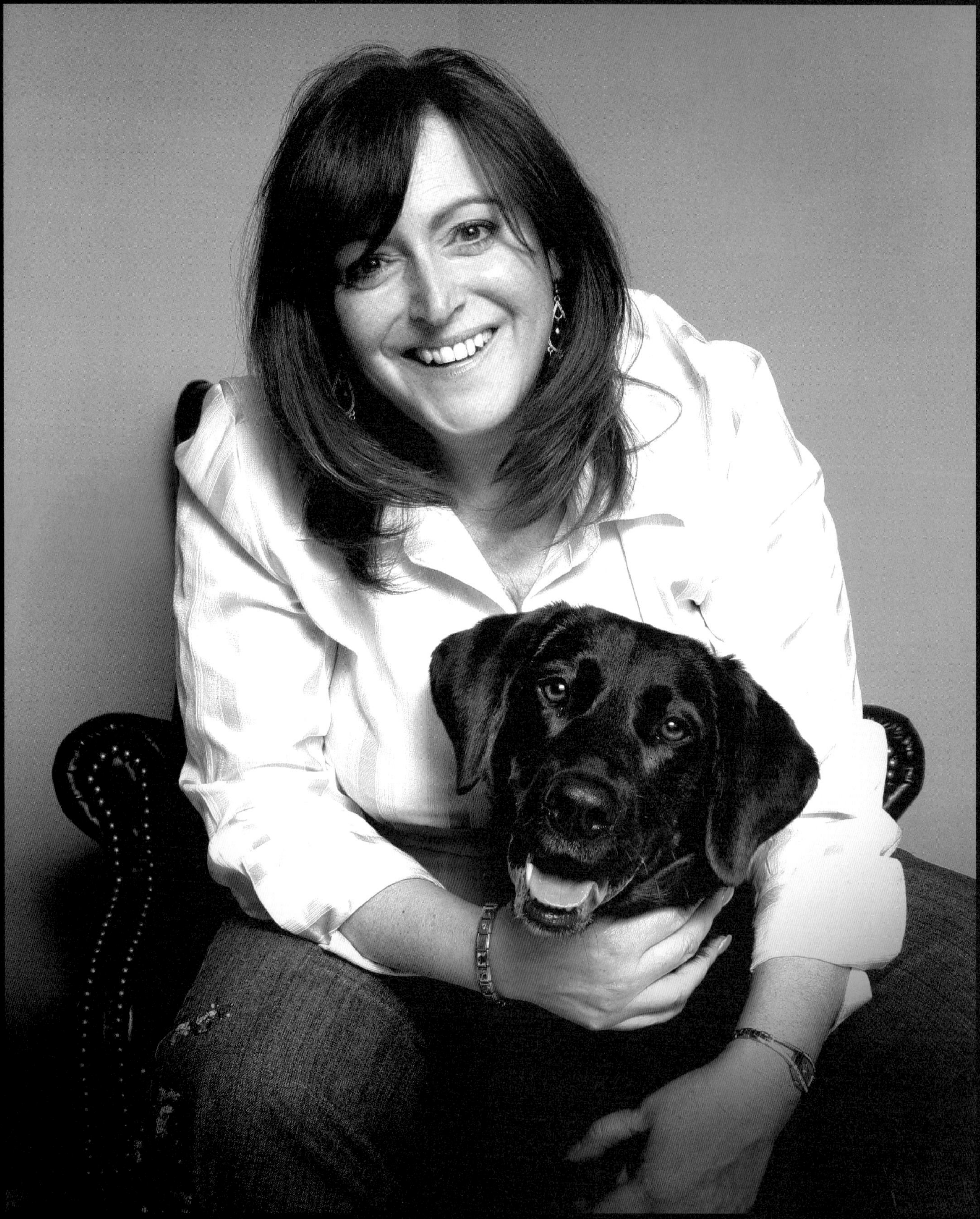

Susan and Misty

Life without Misty would be no fun at all.

He's everyone's dog when he's out and about,

but he always comes home with me.

Christine and Rory

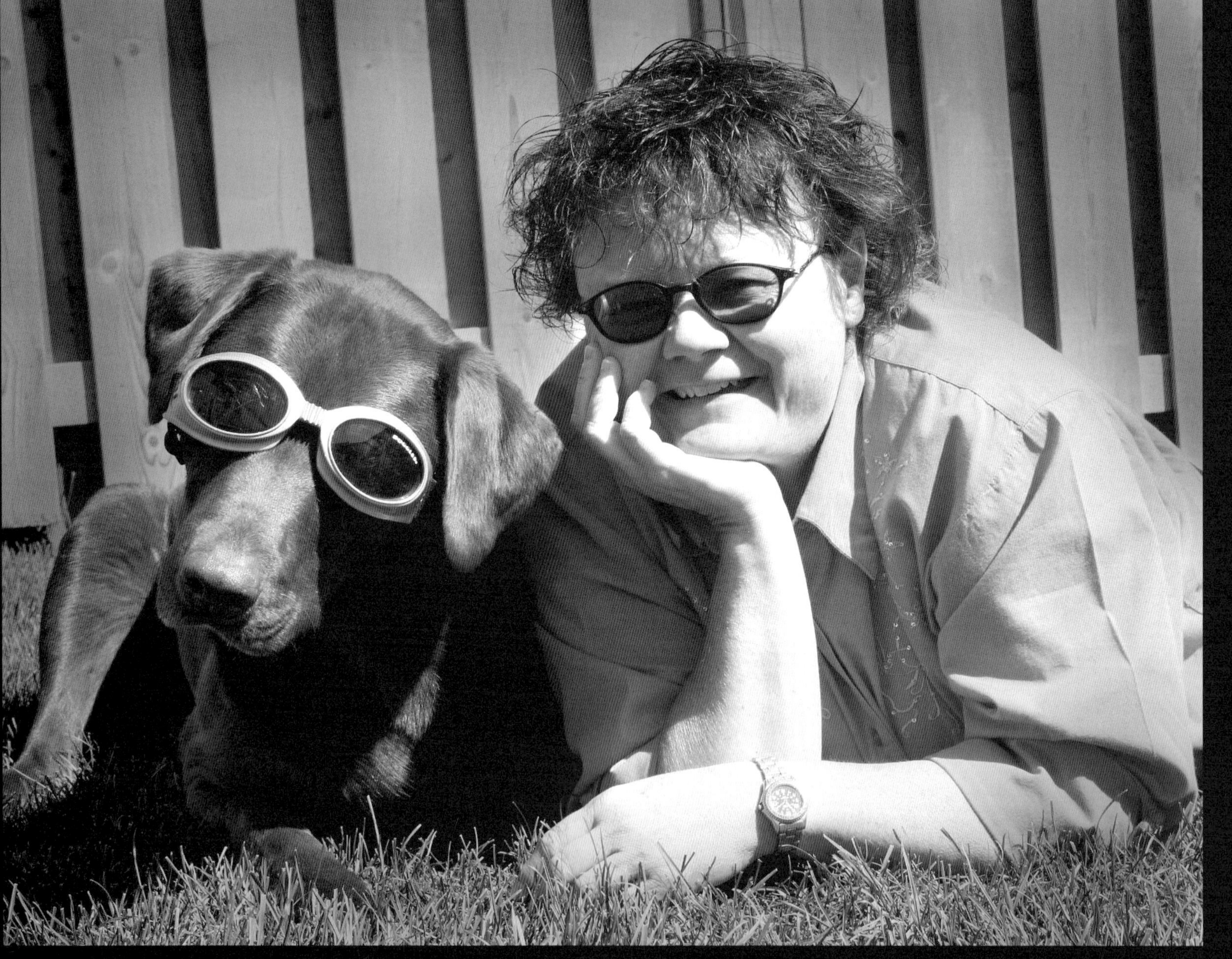

Irene and Moses

At the end of each day,

Moe's kisses help wash away all my stress.

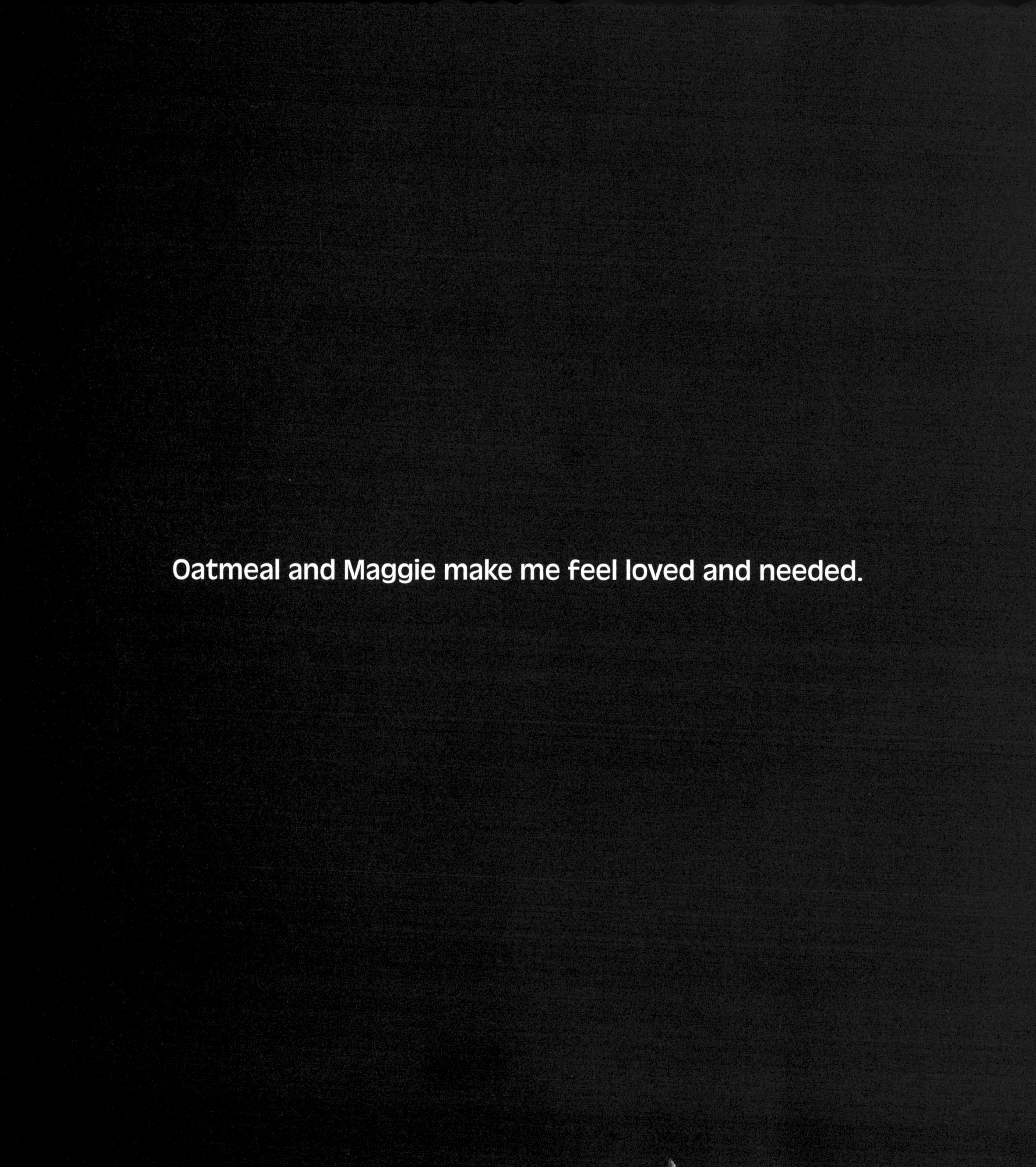


Oatmeal and Maggie make me feel loved and needed.

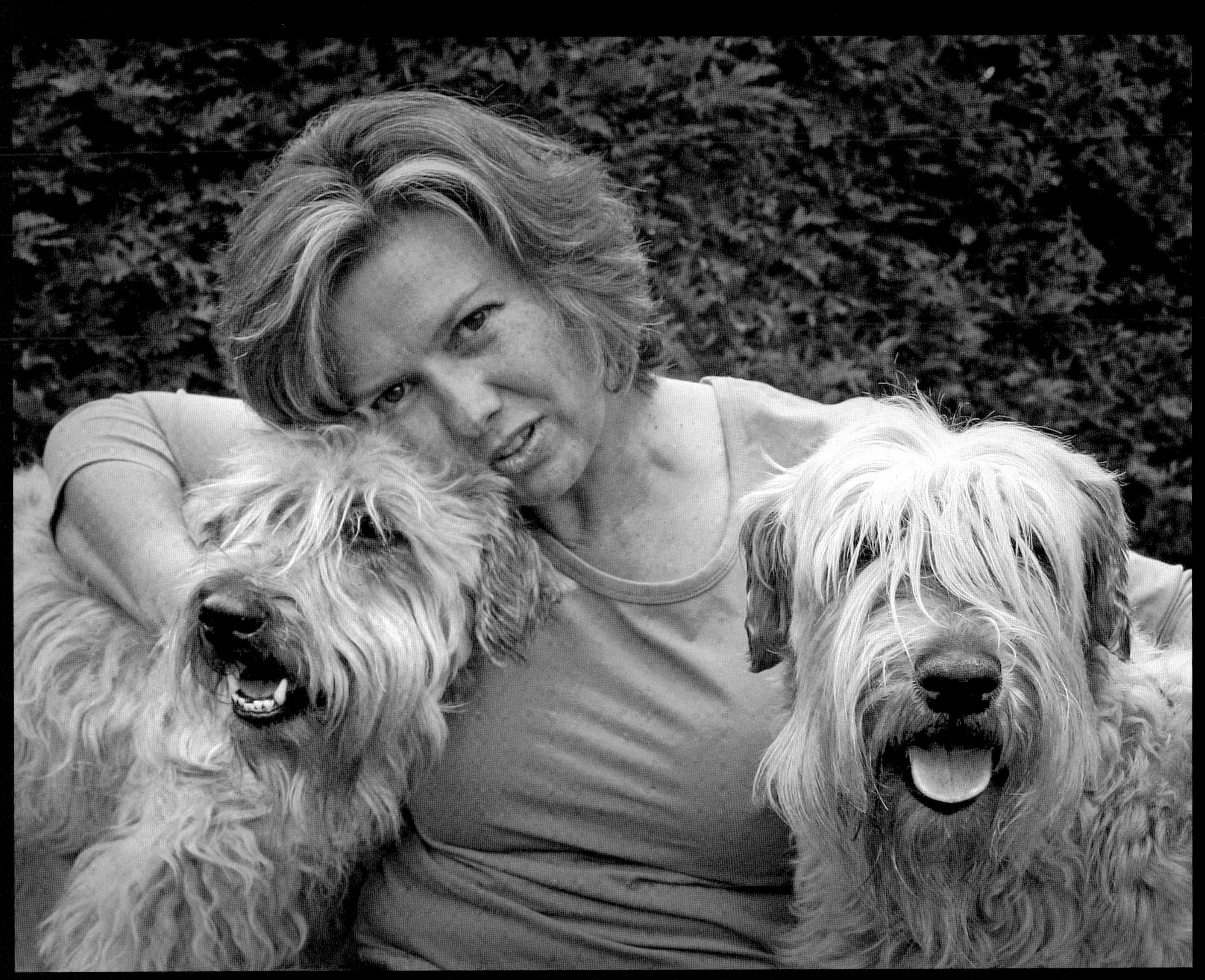

Judy, Oatmeal and Maggie

There is nothing nicer than a grassy field,

a day off work

and a

Golden Retriever named Ike.

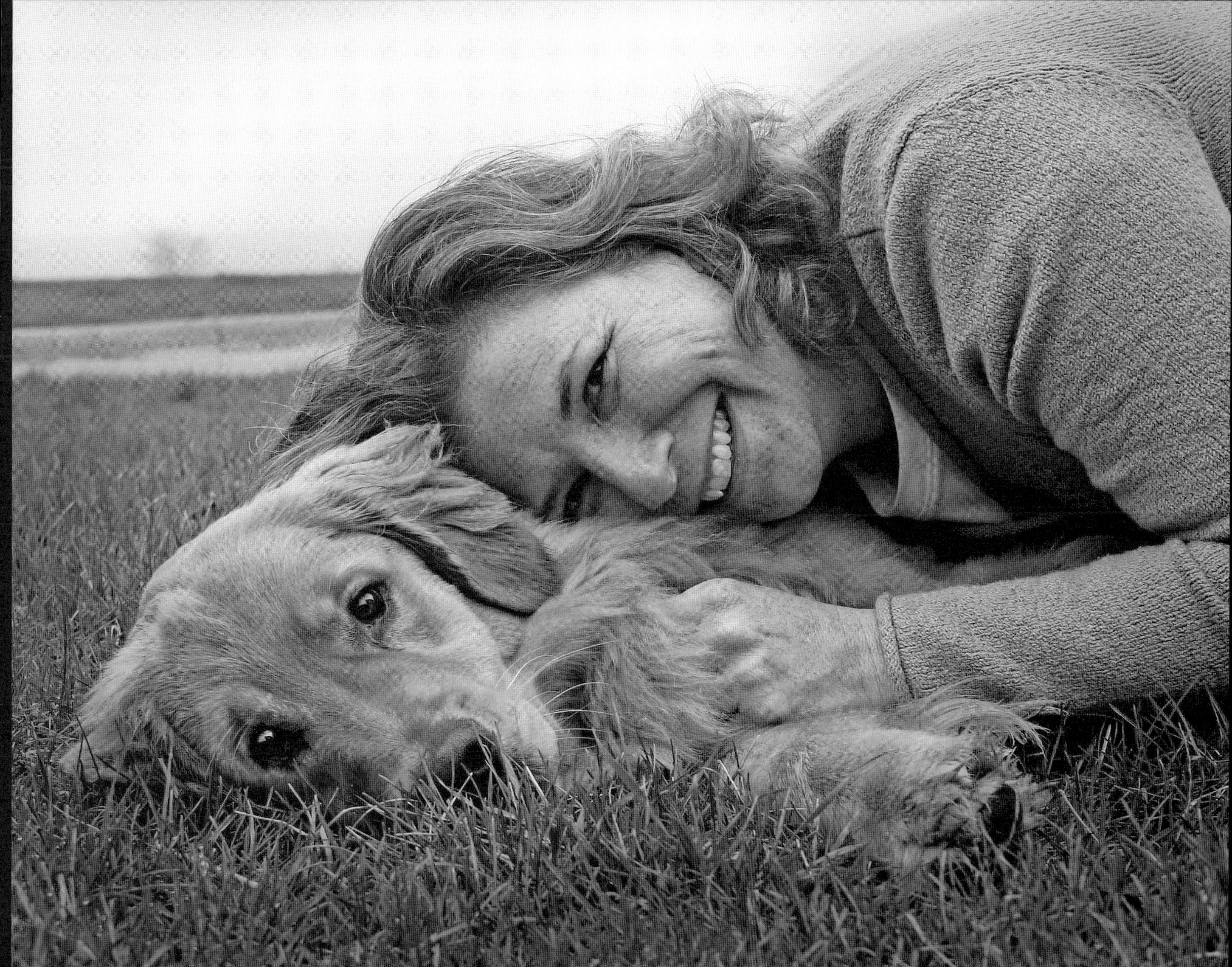

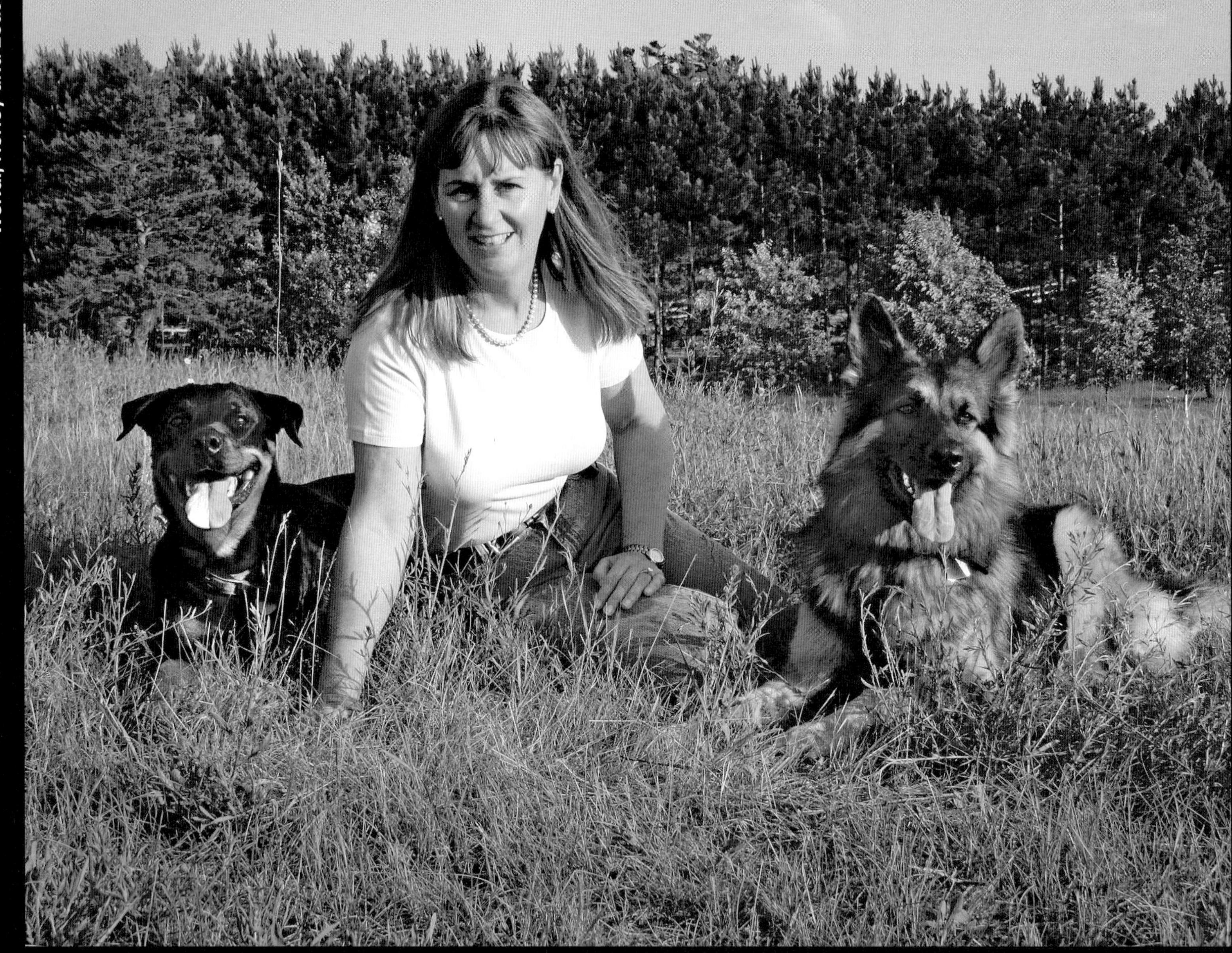



They are my loyal companions who never fail to give me unconditional love

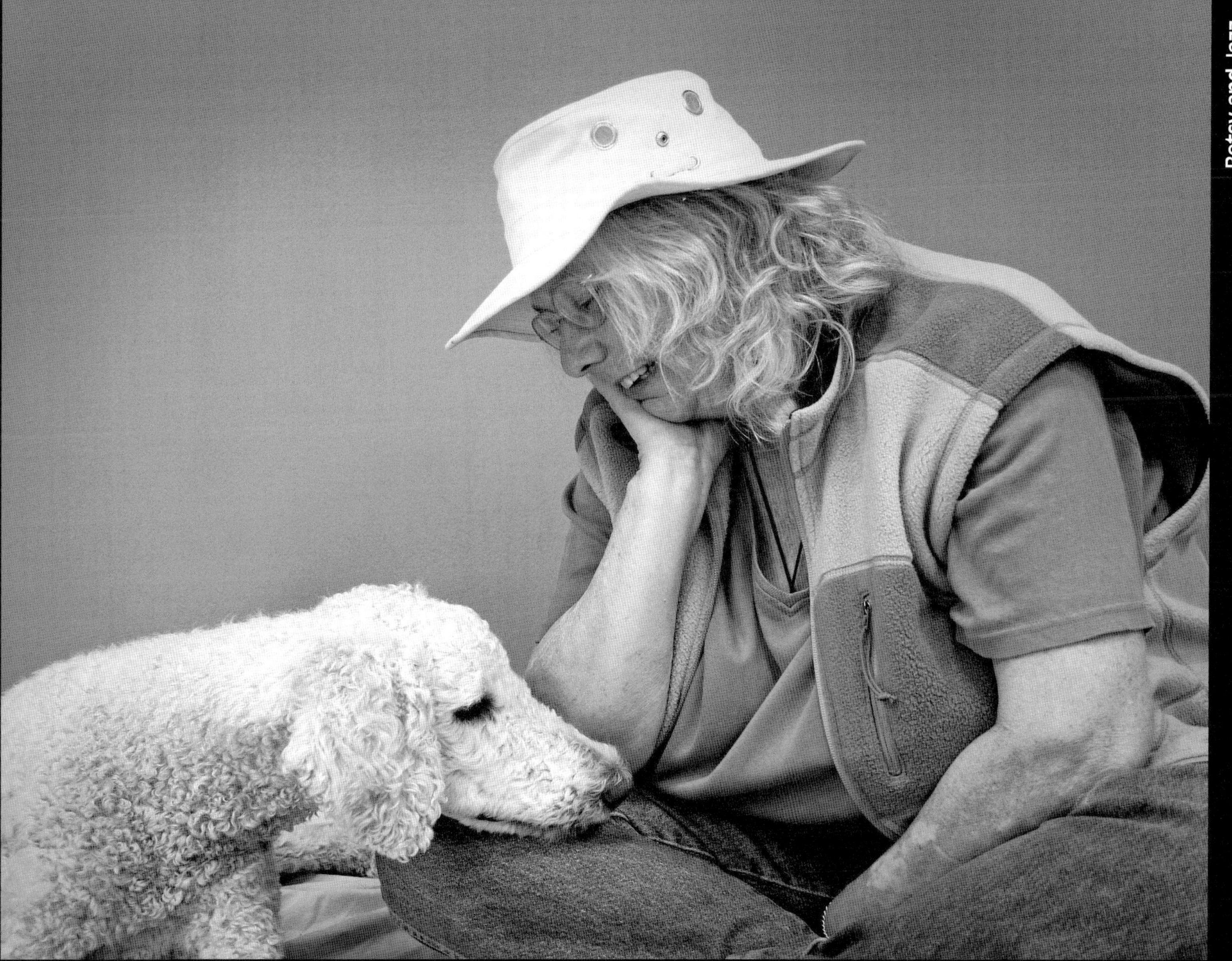


He's 50 pounds of insistence: Play with me!

Great Danes acquire a piece of your heart.

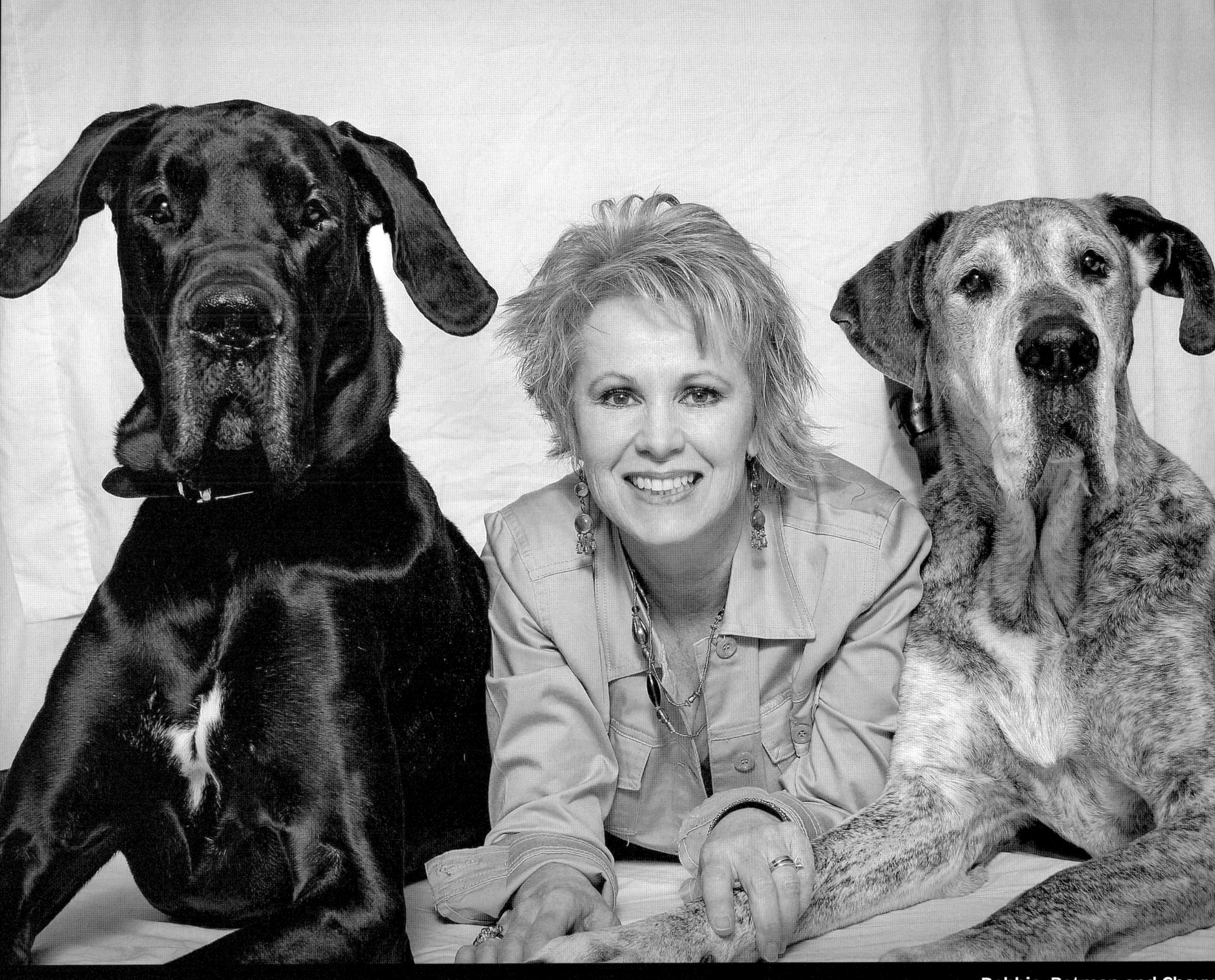

Debbie, Batman and Chevy

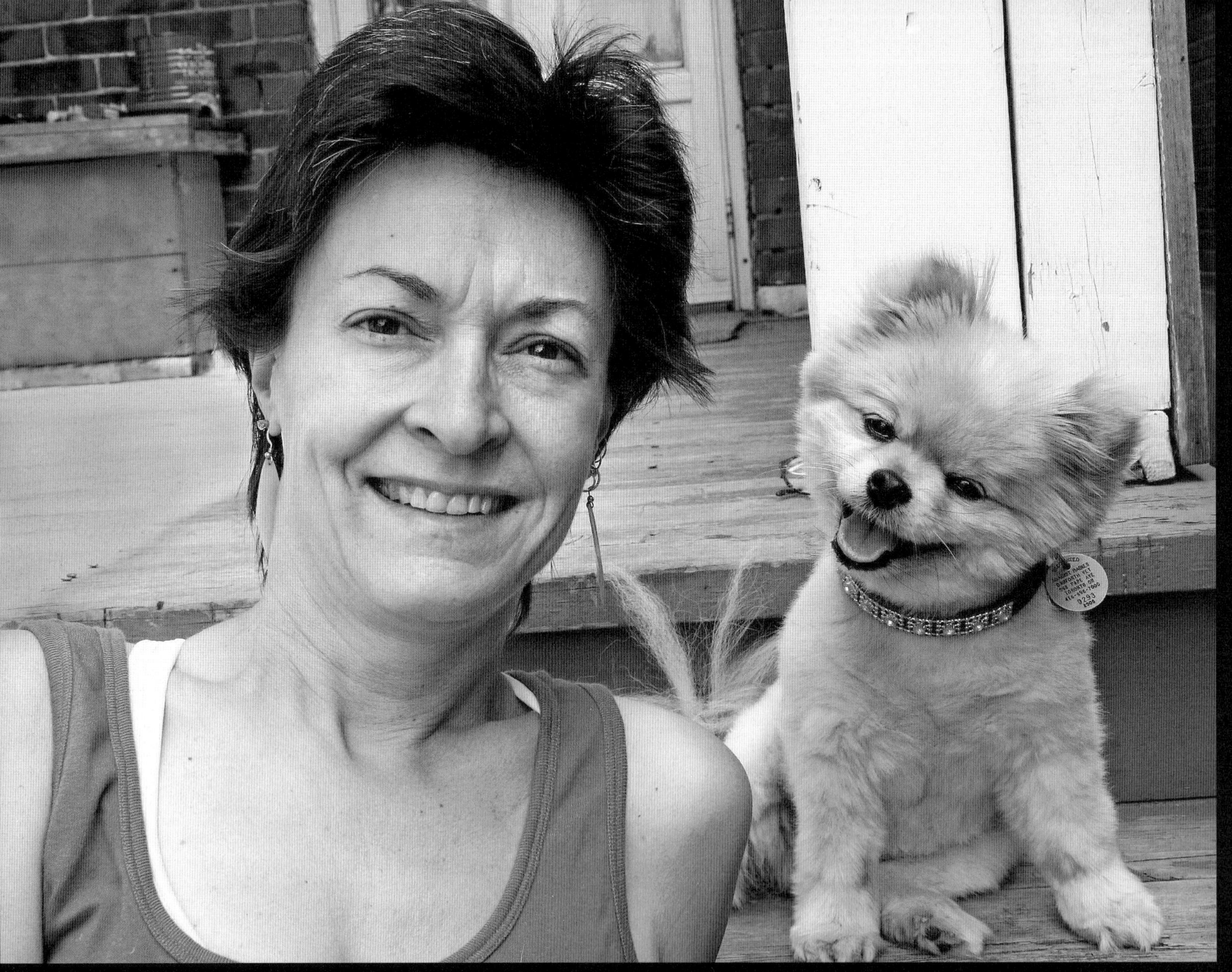

Blanche and Lola

Lola has more gumption and guts than any dog I've ever had.

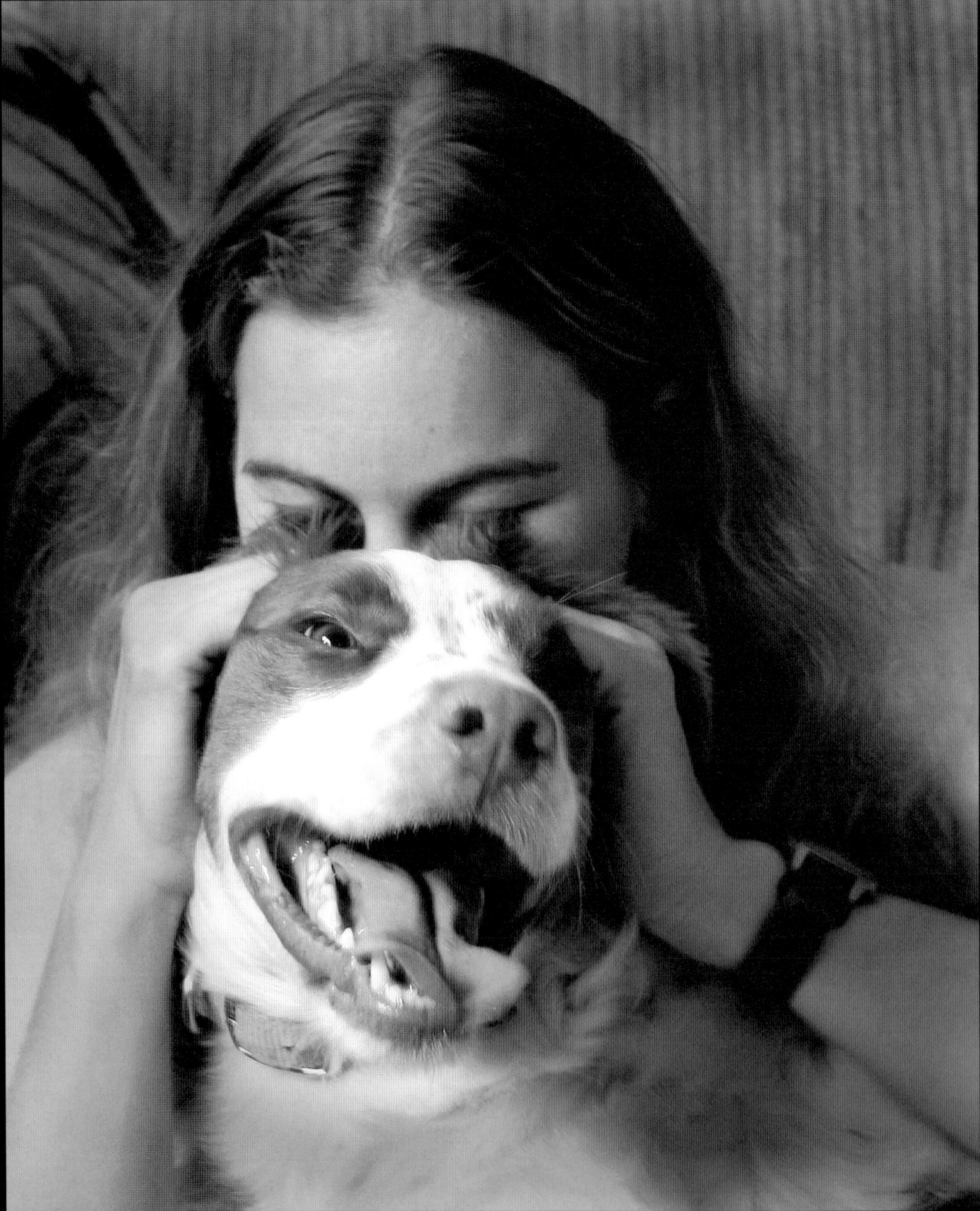

Allison and Reilly

He loves to be anywhere I am.

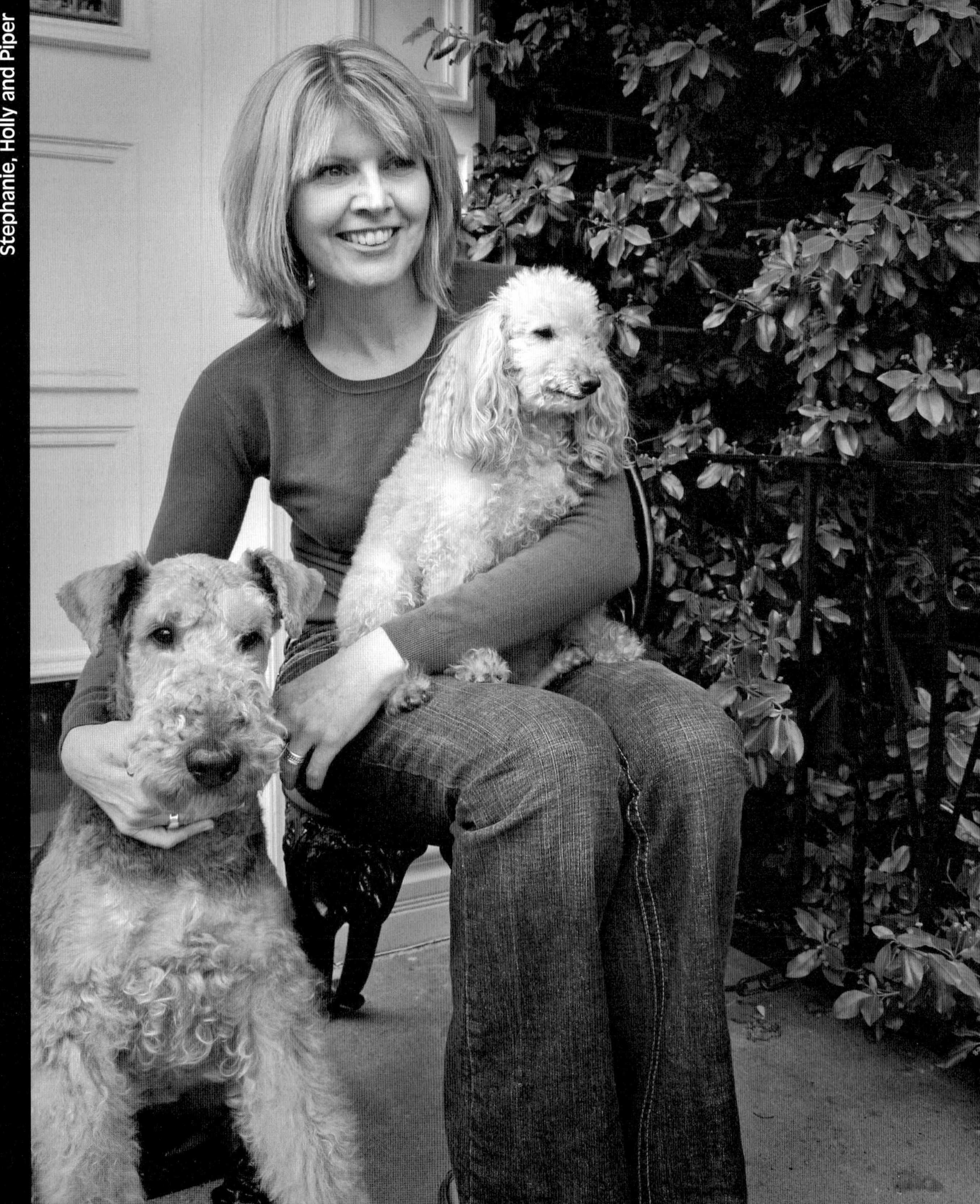


Stephanie, Holly and Piper

These two dogs are as different as can be,

but both offer boundless amounts of love

and every day together

is a gift we cherish.

I call him my angel

because I'm sure

he was sent to me from above.

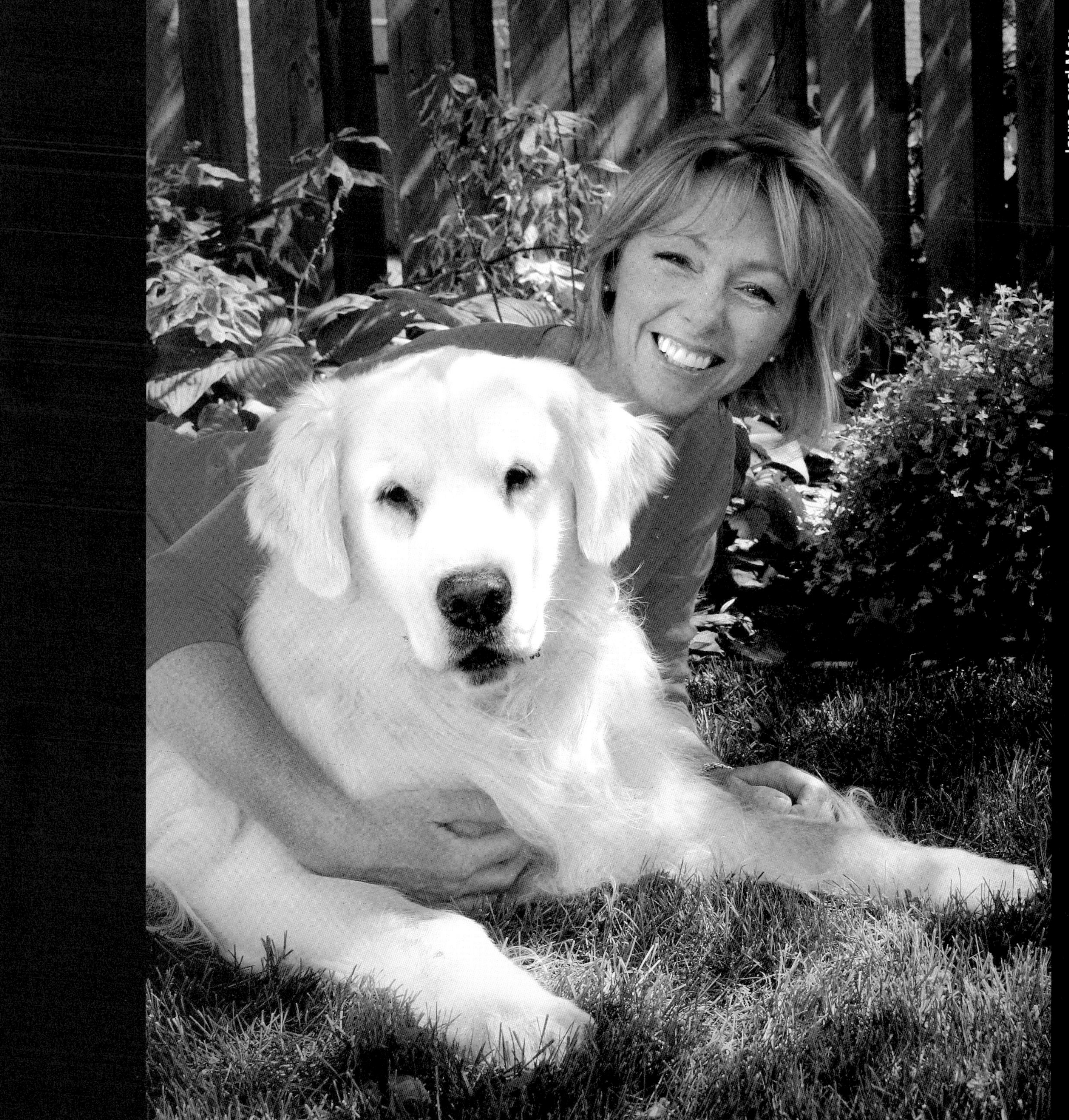

Jayne and Max

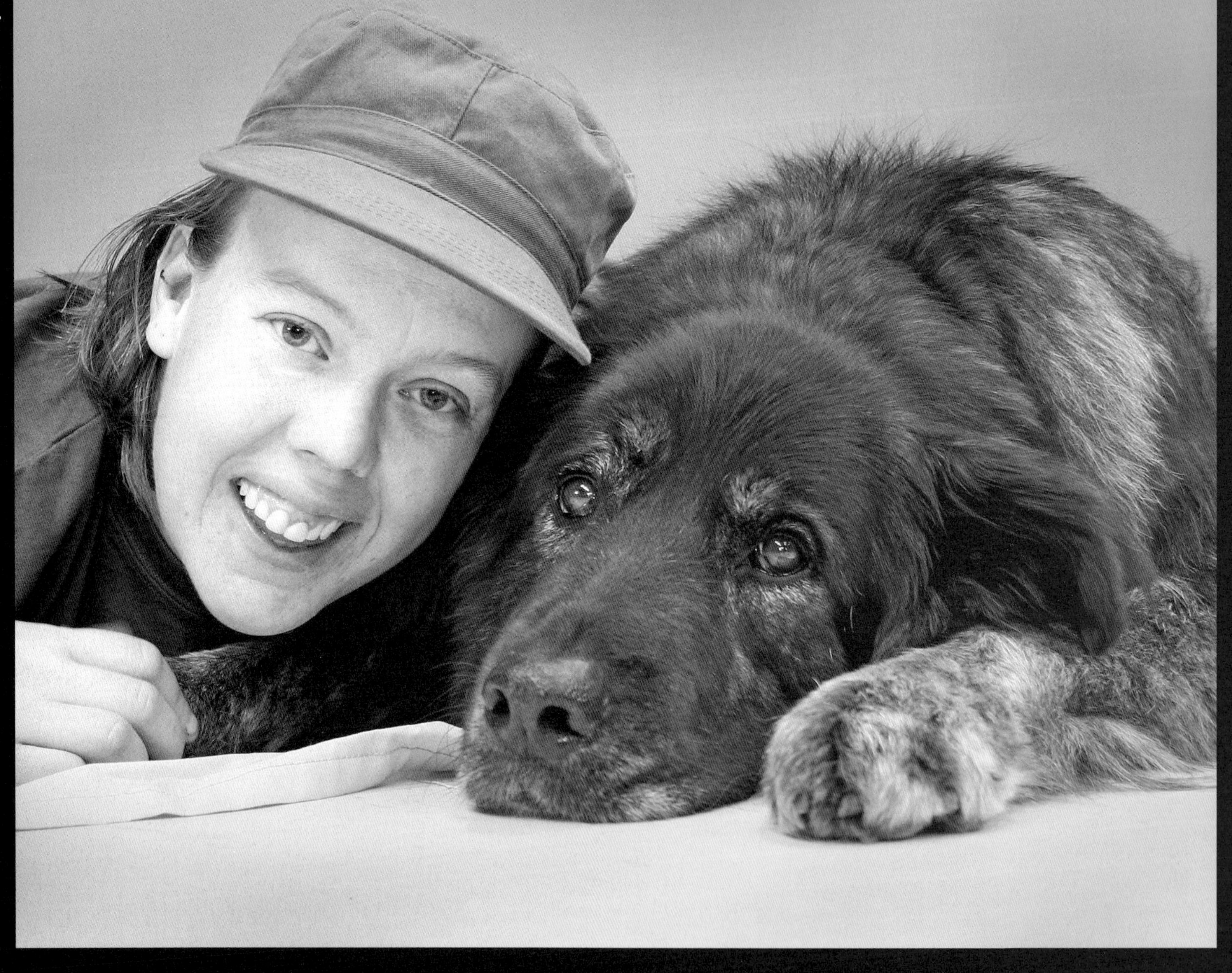



We both suffer separation anxiety when we are not together.

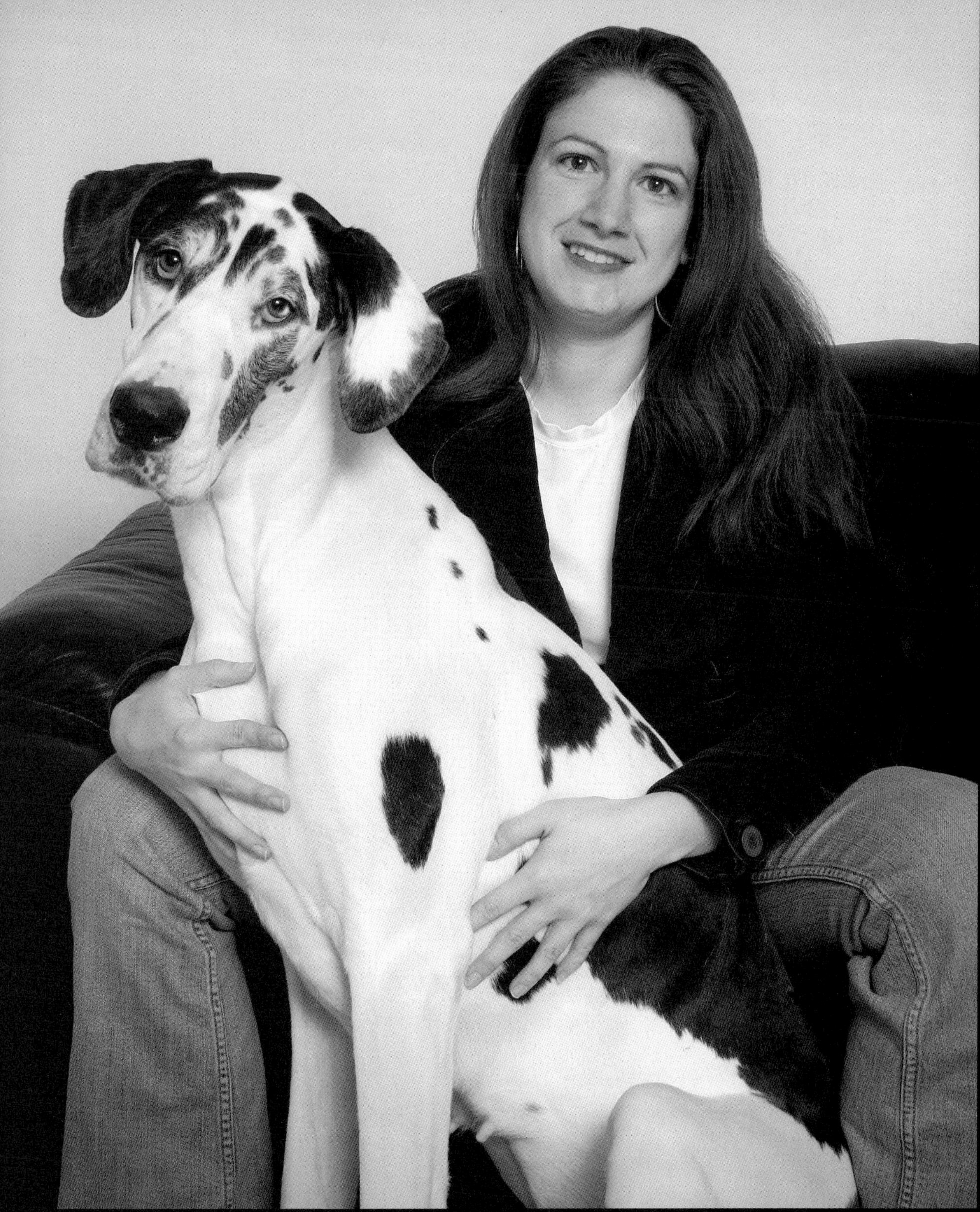


Mary and Jazzy

A nine-month-old puppy,

a nine-week-old puppy

and

I'm nine months pregnant.

I think I will need nine arms to help me!

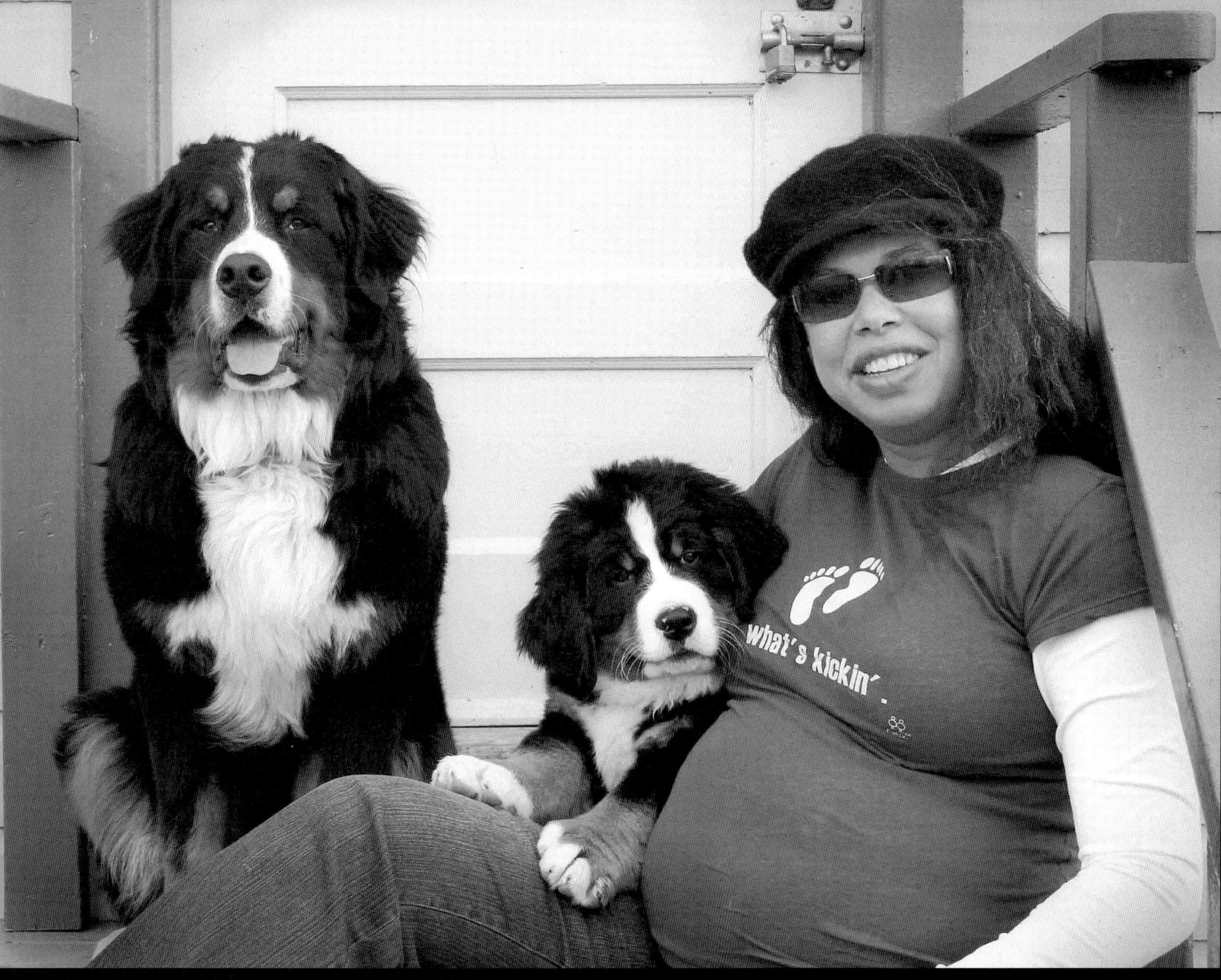

Shawn, Duke and Tiny

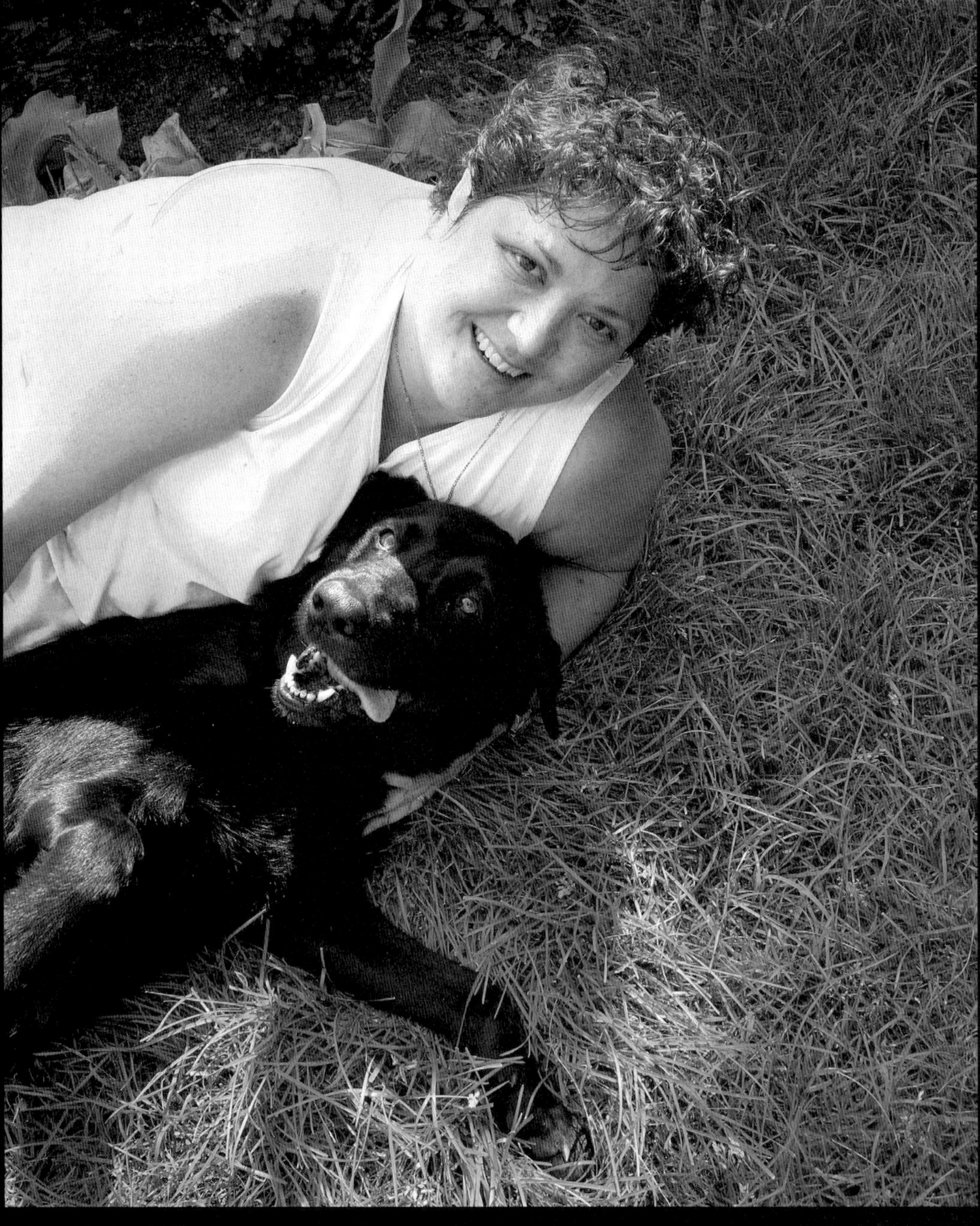

Connie and Nivek

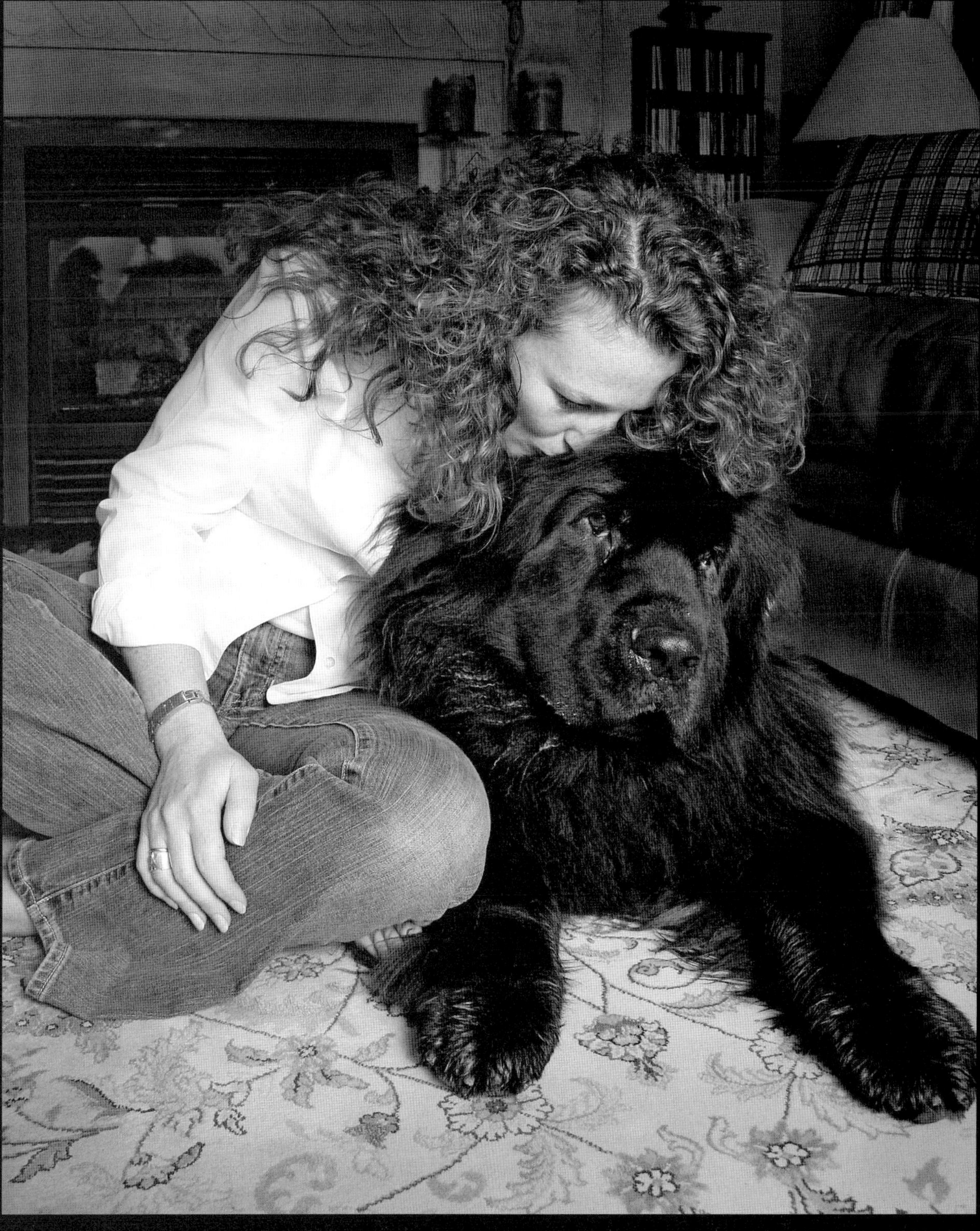

Joanna and Ned

Abby was born on

Valentine's Day.

How fitting, because

she's stolen

my heart.

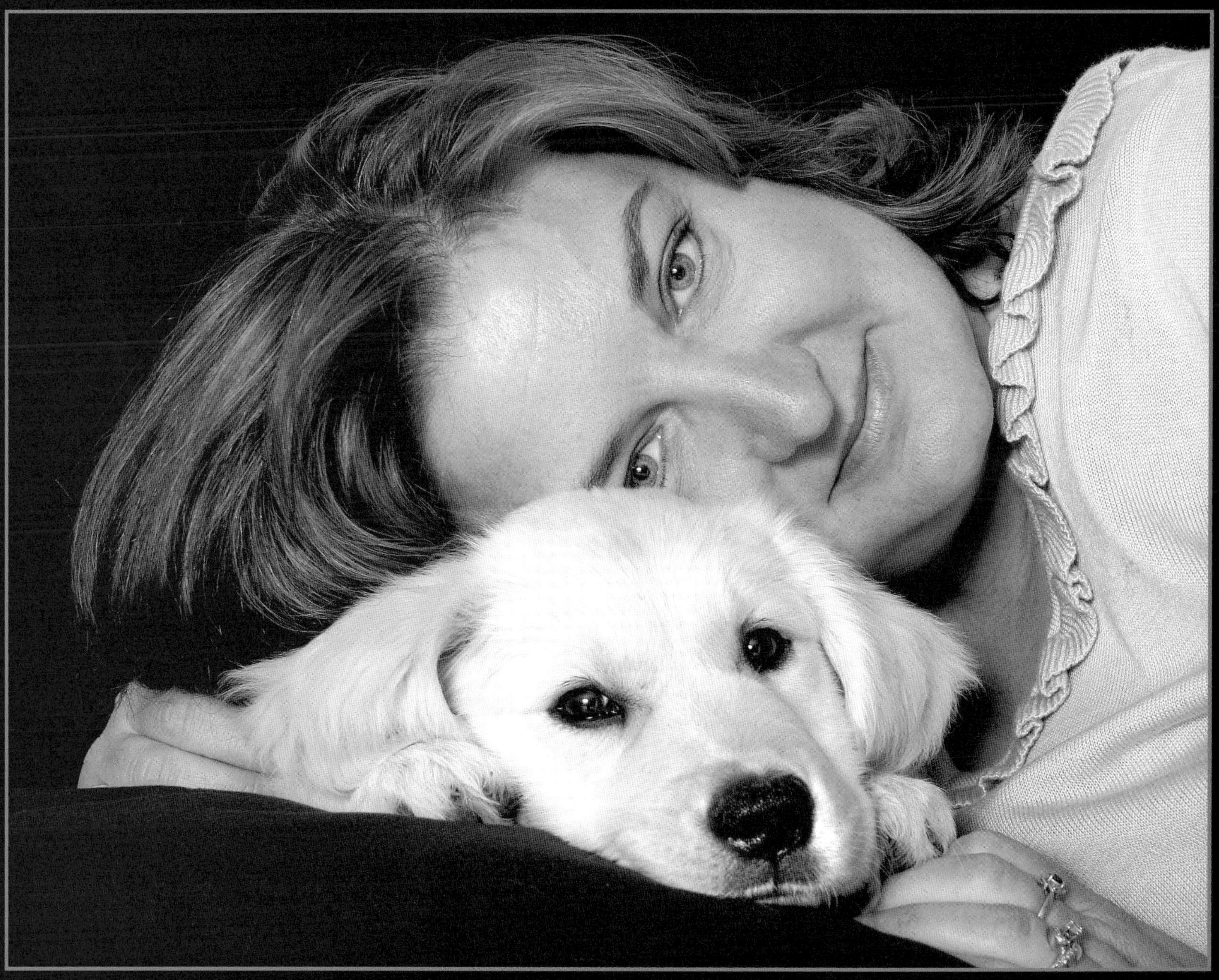

Jackie and Abby

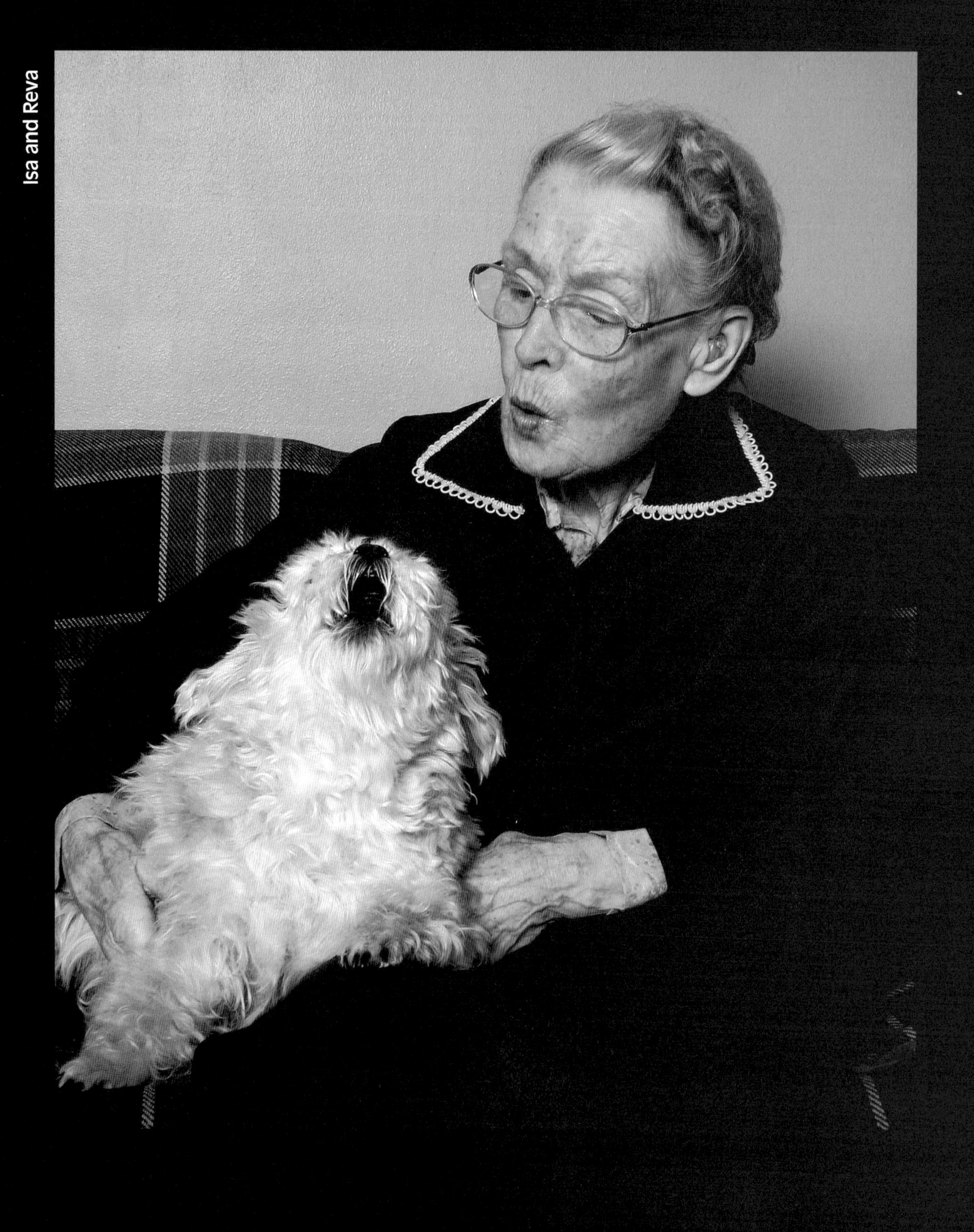

Isa and Reva

Reva is an angel sent from God,

and has a holy howl to prove it.

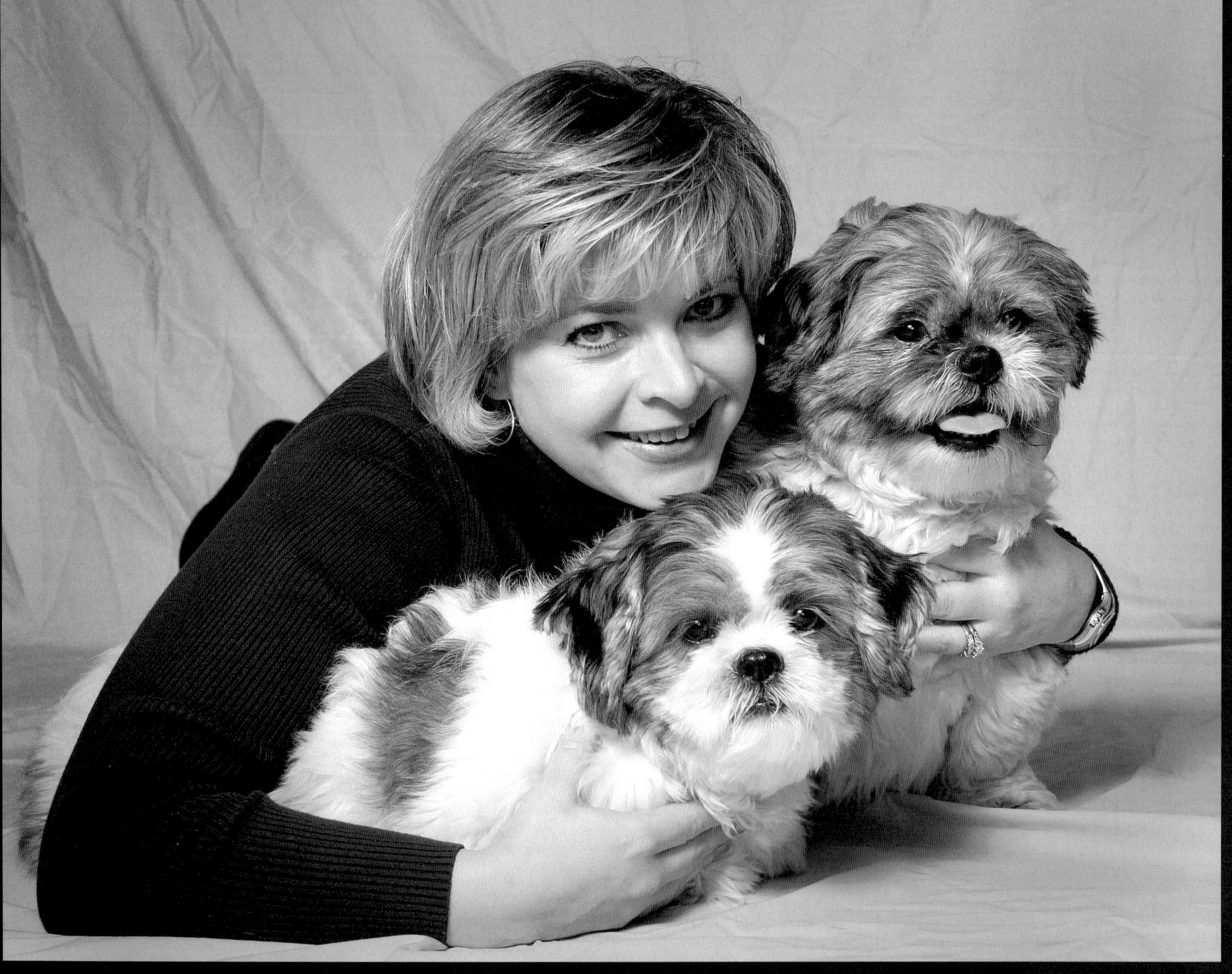

Shelley, Brodie and Albie

We enjoy car rides and long walks together.

But most of all, we just love to cuddle.

Bailey's eyes are the window to her soul.

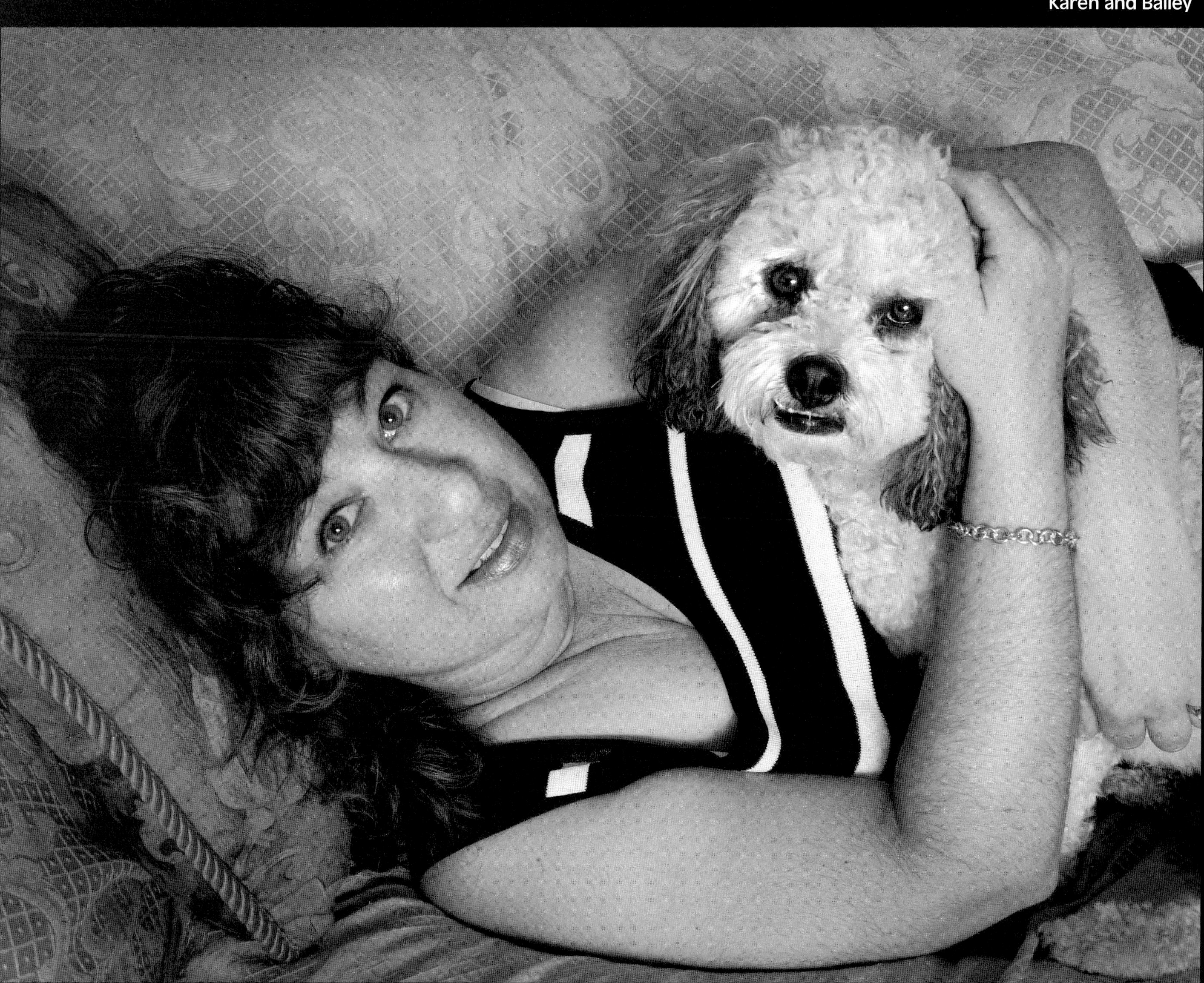
Karen and Bailey

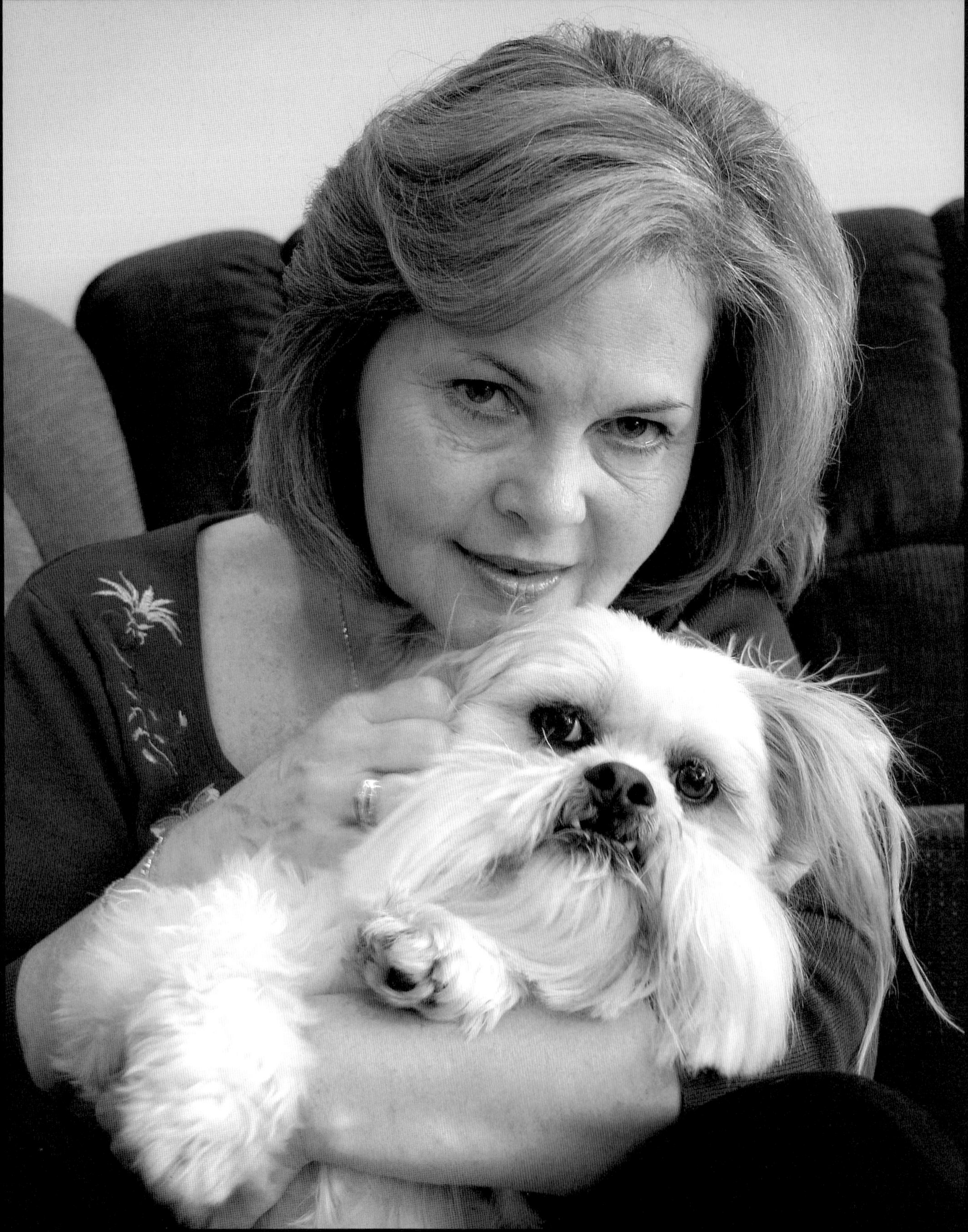

Sussan and Bandit

Bandit stole my heart

and became

my shadow,

my guardian

and companion.

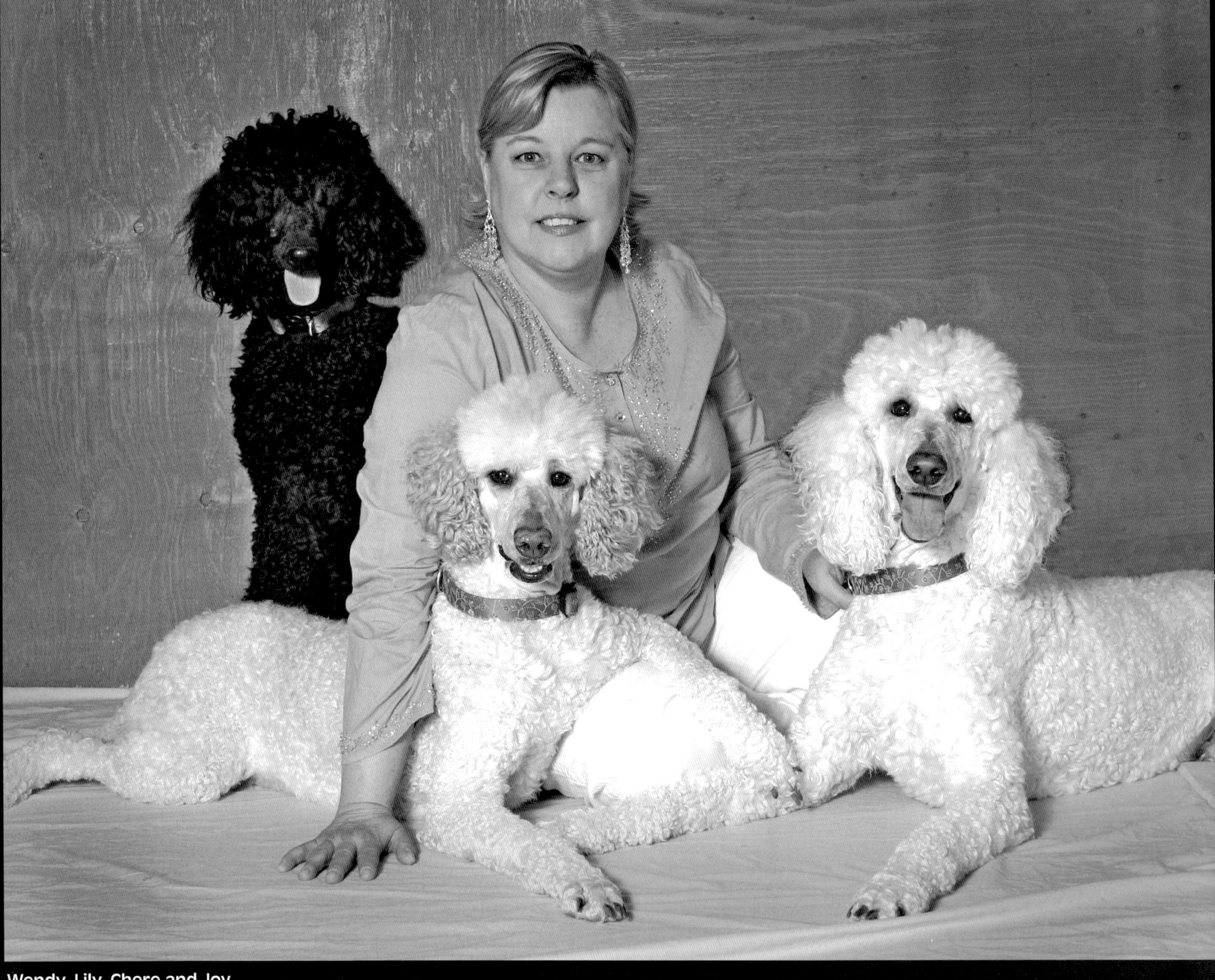

Wendy, Lily, Chere and Joy

Don't let their genteel looks fool you.

These farm girls

love to hang out with the horses

in their paddocks

or run full speed

through the forest.

Barney and I are always together.

He's my co-worker,

my bodyguard

and my best buddy.

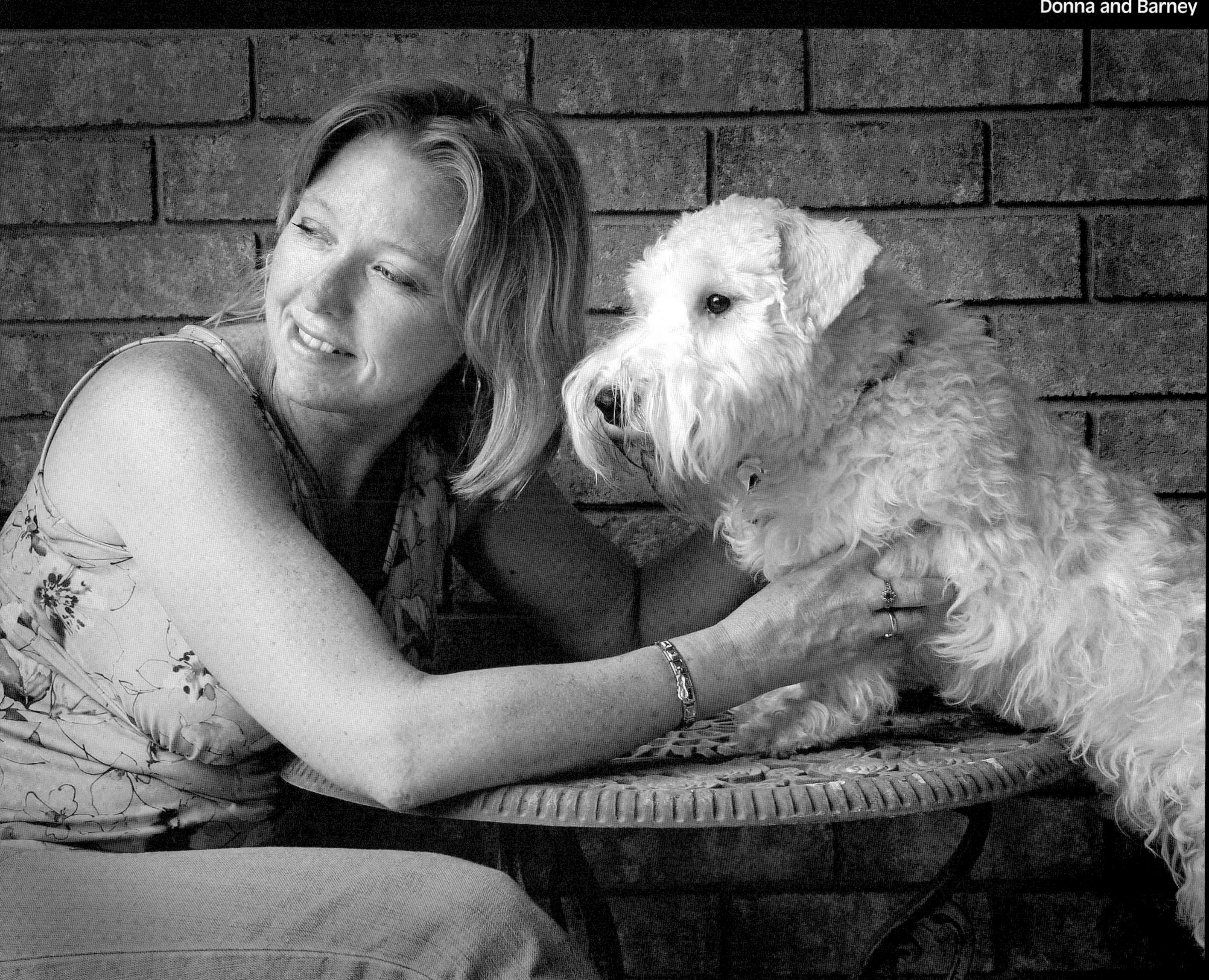
Donna and Barney

His soulful eyes

mask a mischievous sprite.

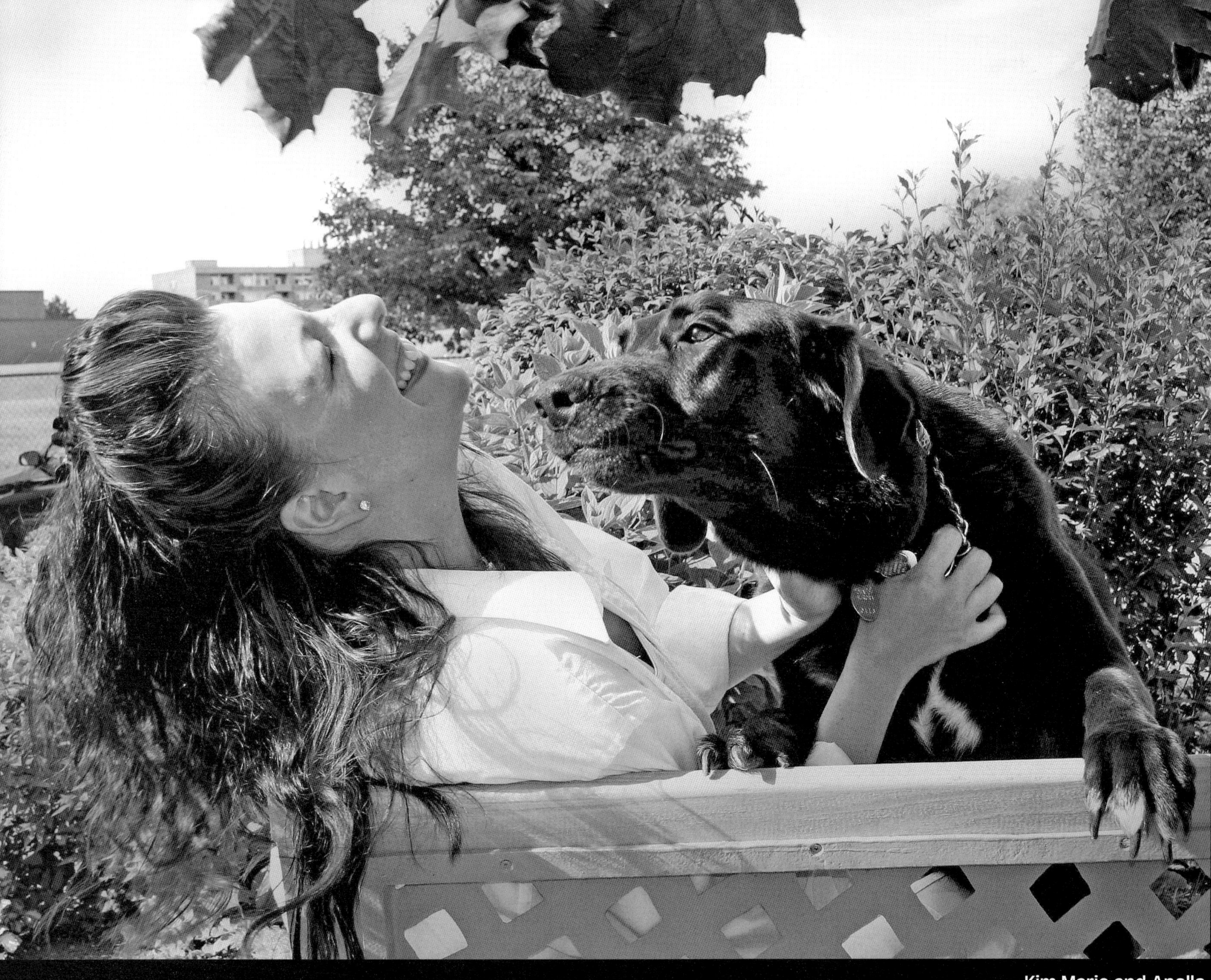

Kim-Marie and Apollo

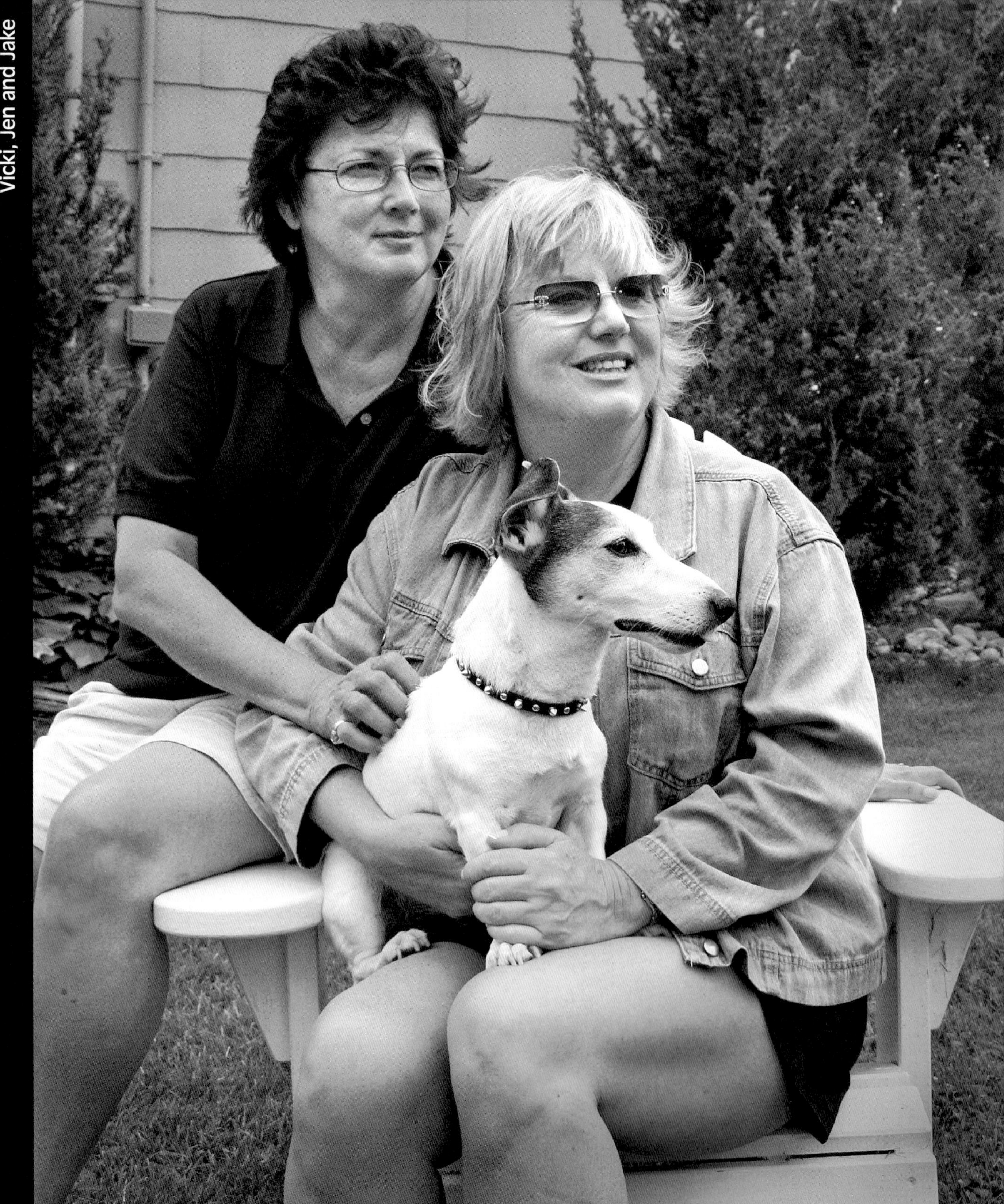
Vicki, Jen and Jake

Life is more fun and interesting

when you share it with an affectionate,

stubborn and very cool dog.

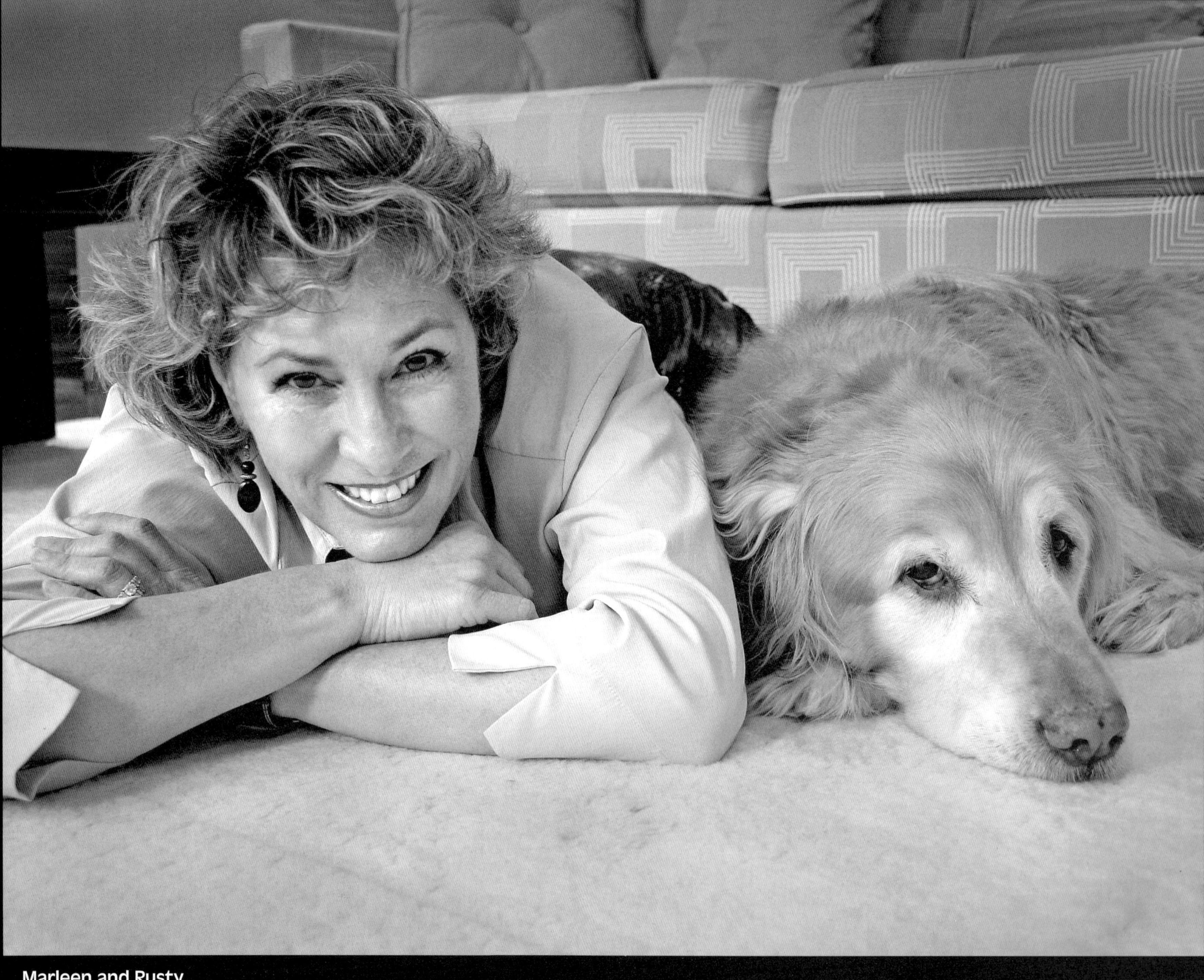

Marleen and Rusty

Rusty was always more of a porch dog
than a real retriever.

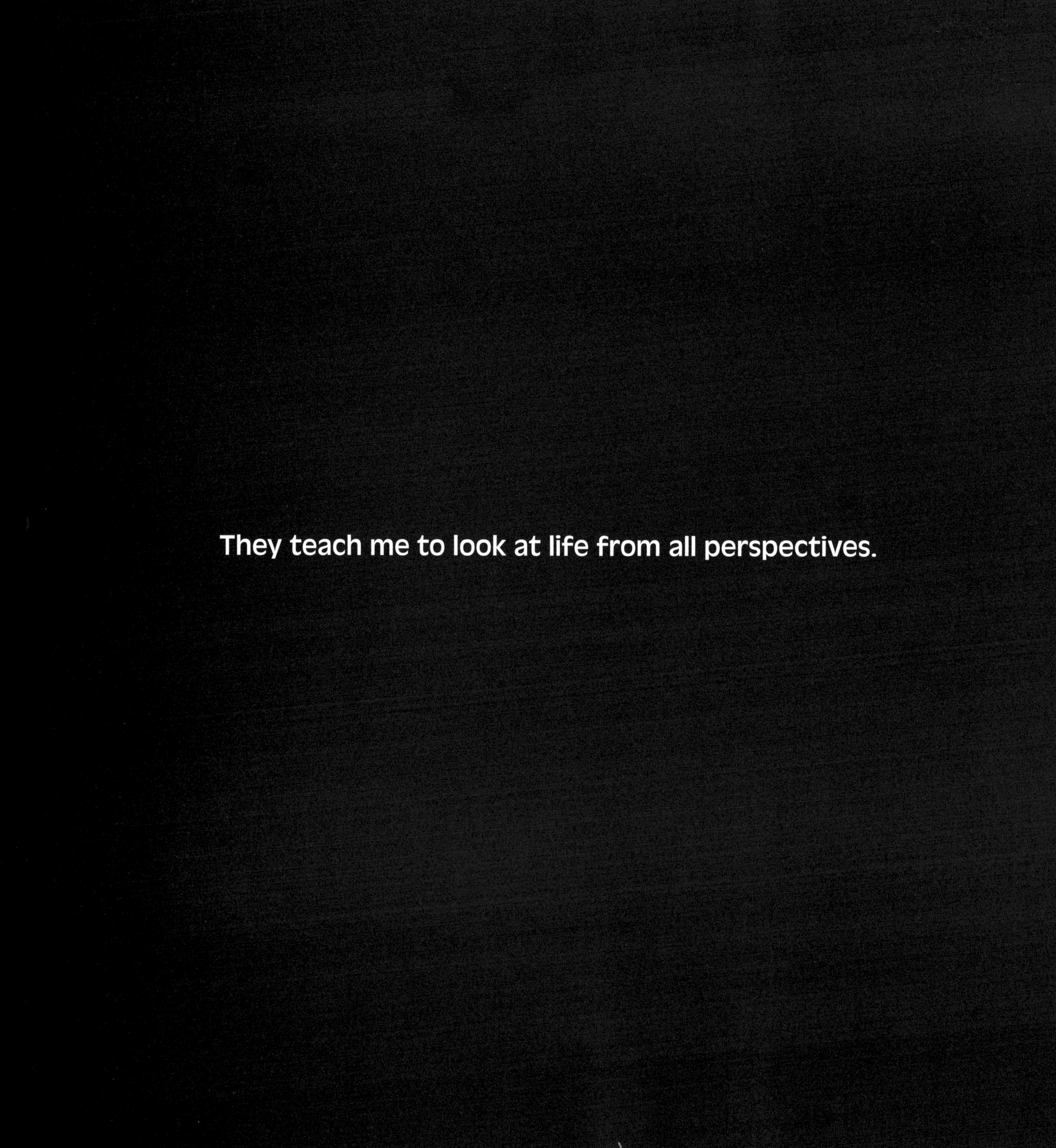


They teach me to look at life from all perspectives.

Susan, Jake and Molly

Who could possibly resist this face?

Not me!

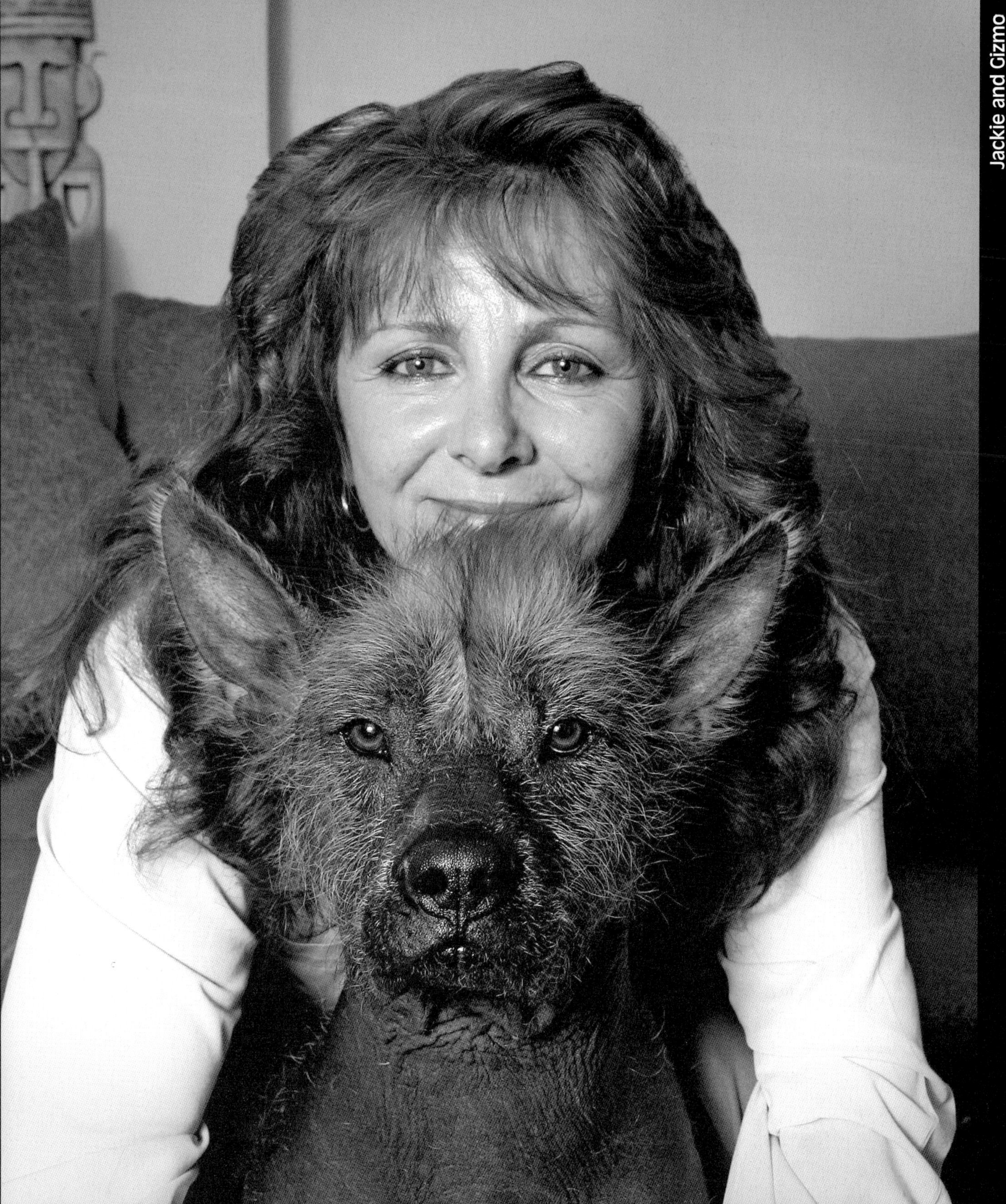
Jackie and Gizmo

Most days it's hard to know

who is more dependant on whom,

but the love is clearly mutual.

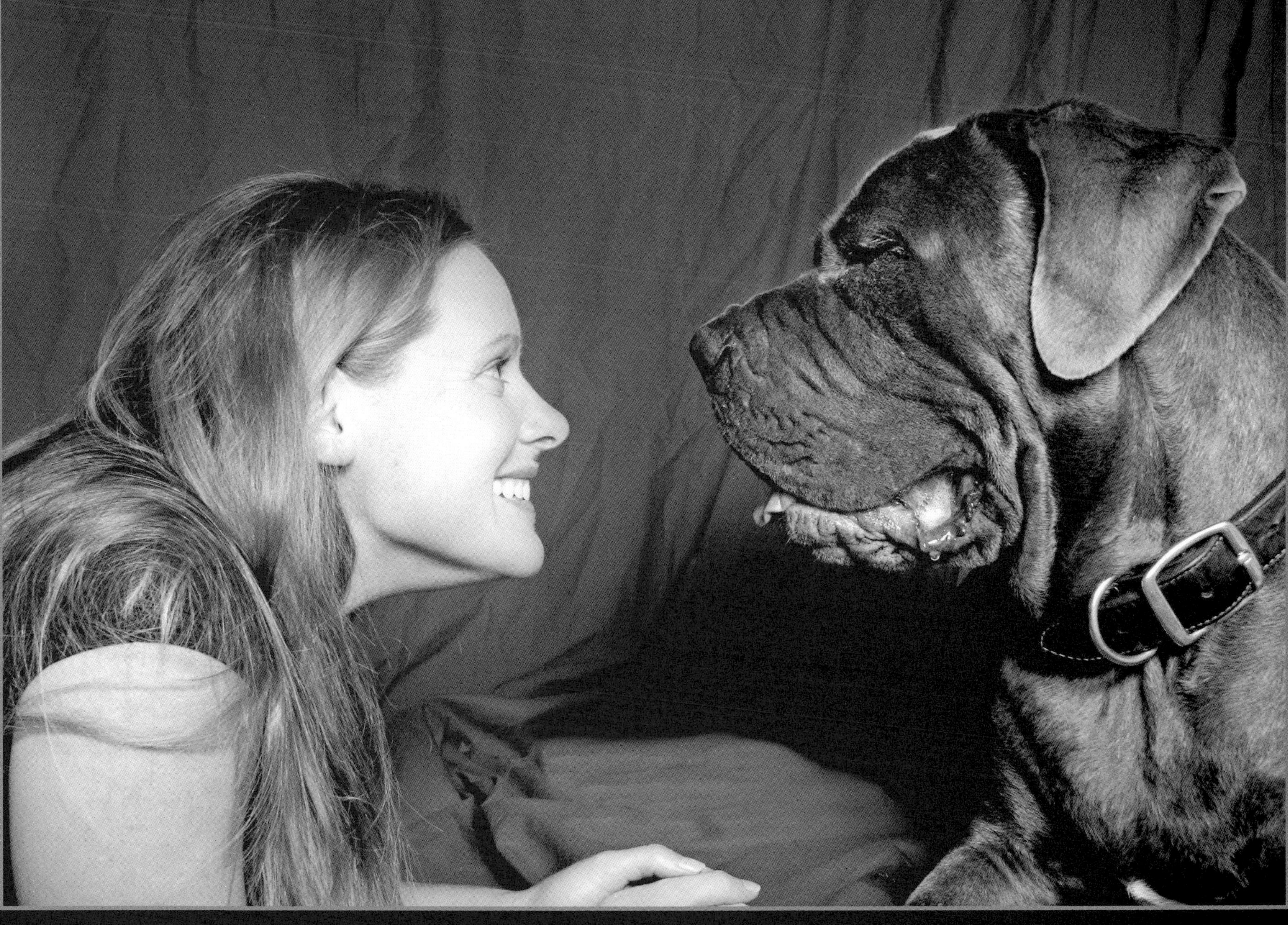

Alexis and Navy

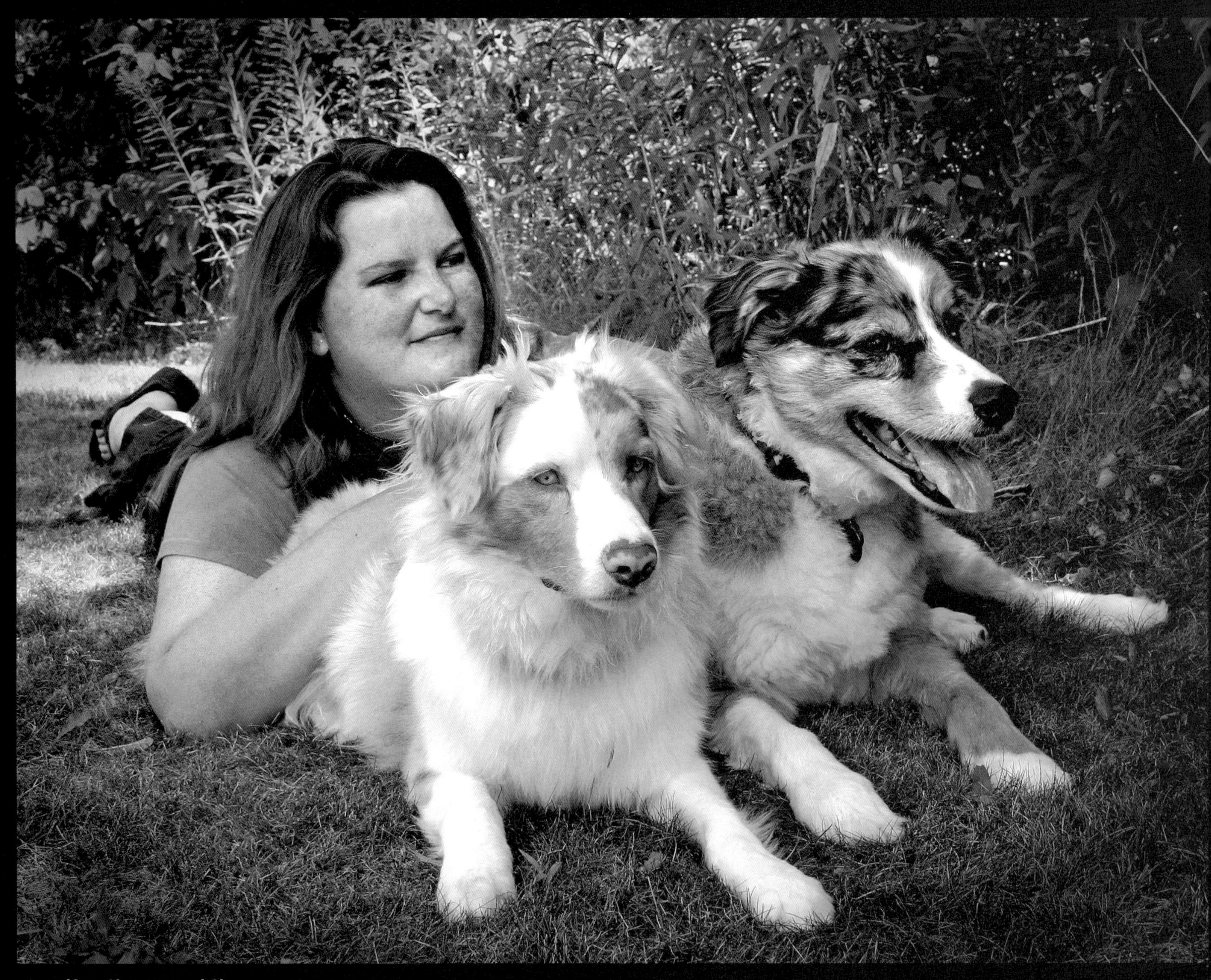

Jennifer, Chance and Sky

After eating everything

from my sunglasses to a bottle of Advil,

I've learned patience is a virtue

and having your vet's number on speed dial is a must.

Earl was abandoned

but has found

his new and forever home.

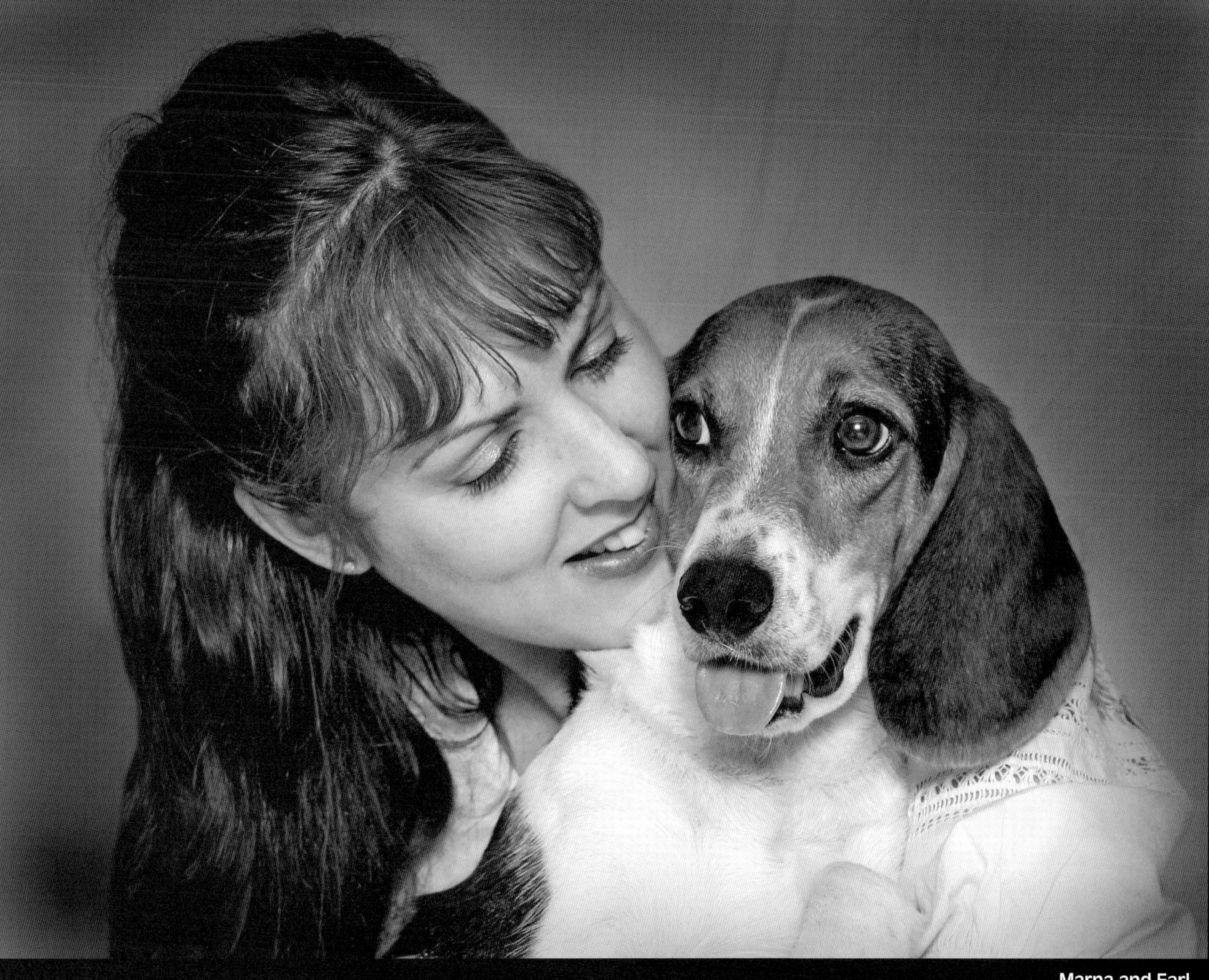

Marna and Earl

Tess reminds me

to laugh, love and roll in the dirt

every once in a while.

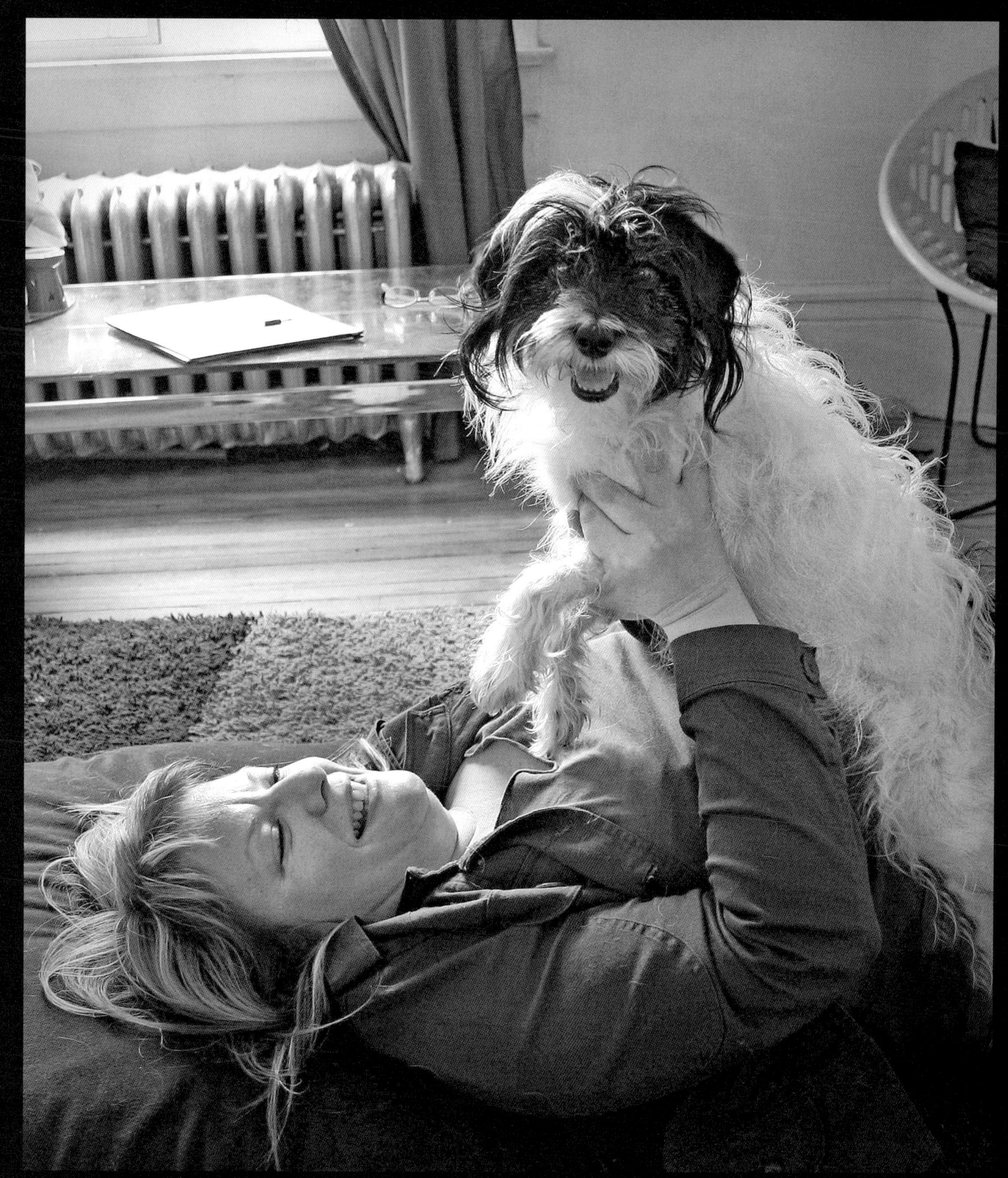

Sandy and Tess

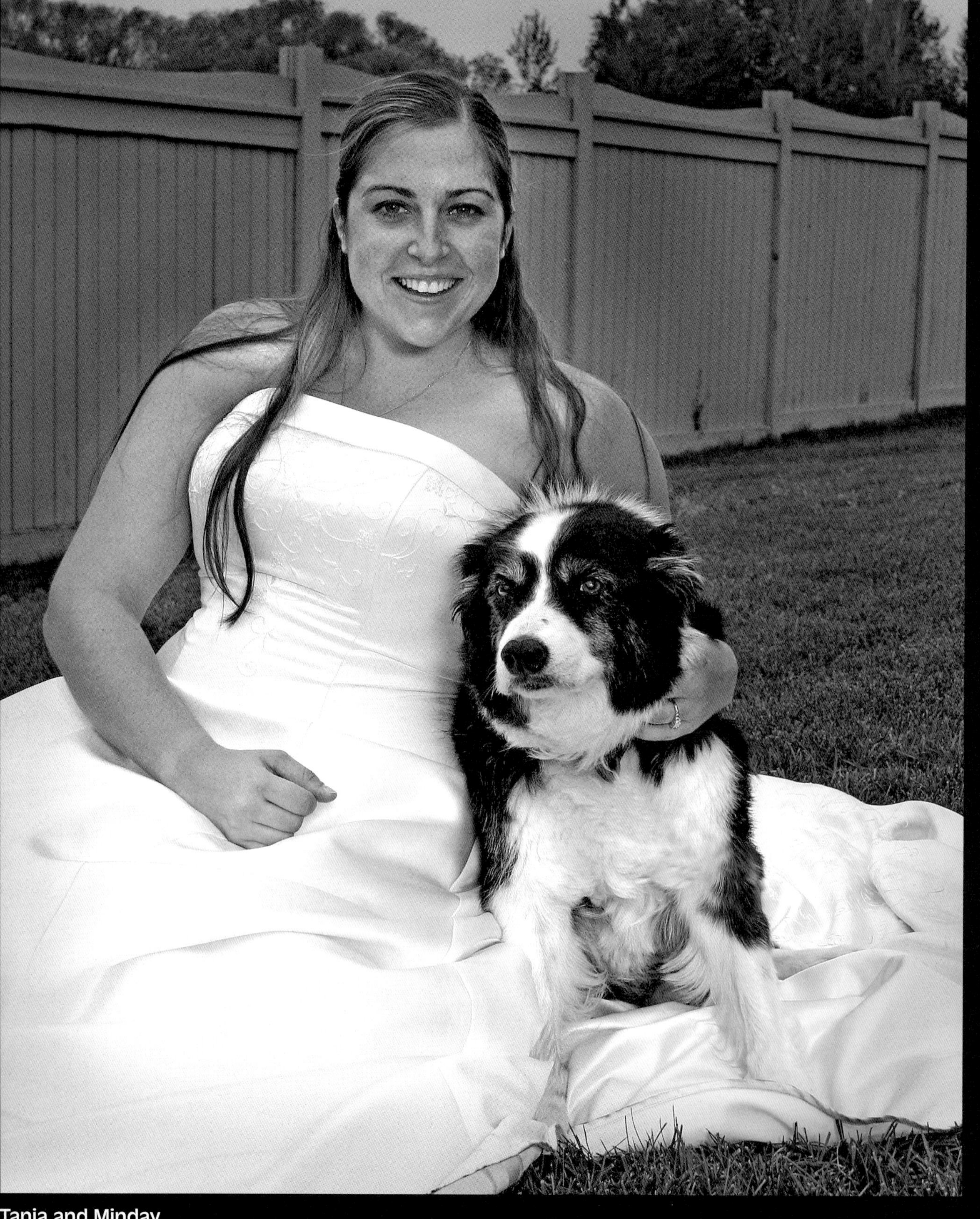


Tania and Minday

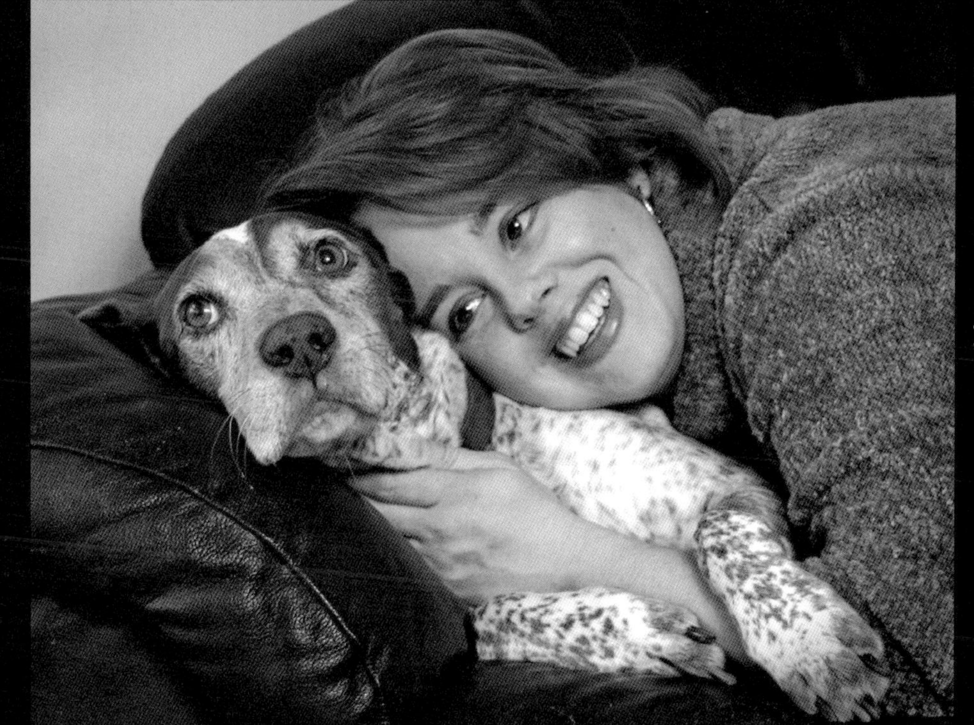



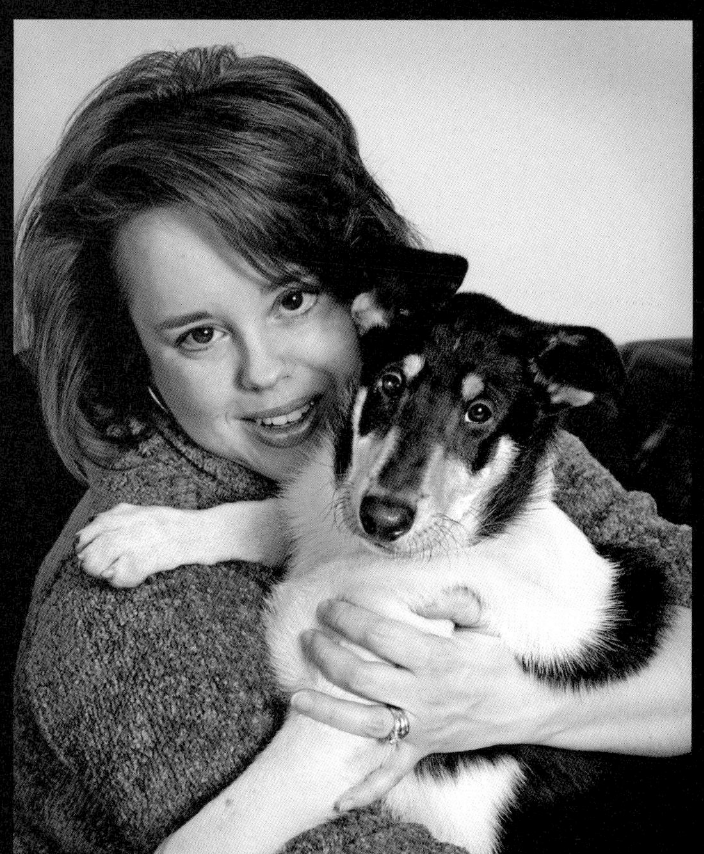

There is nothing like

sharing space with

someone you love.

These are the best noses

for pressing up against the window

to greet me after a hard day at work.

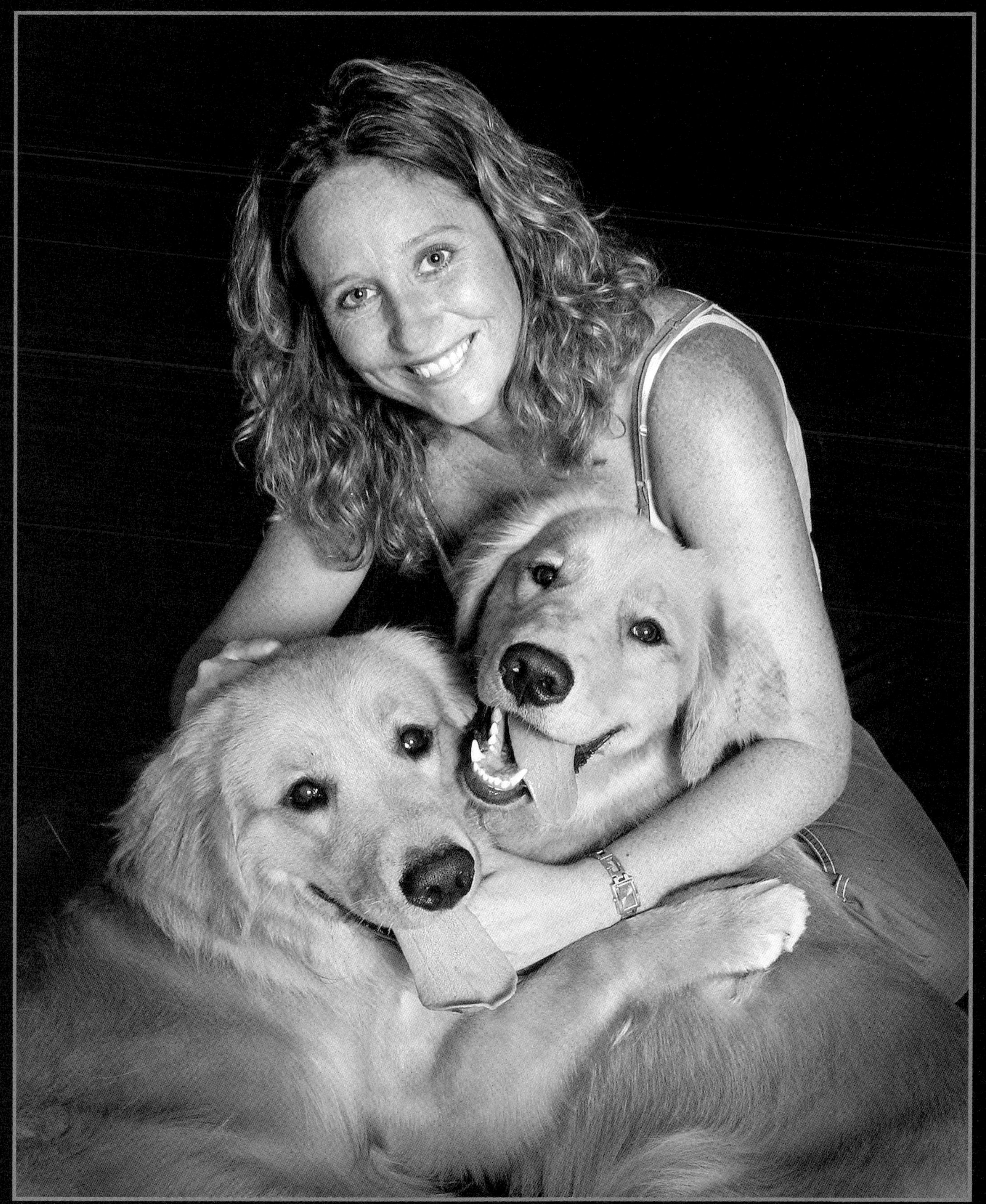

Lyndsey, Sam and Scout

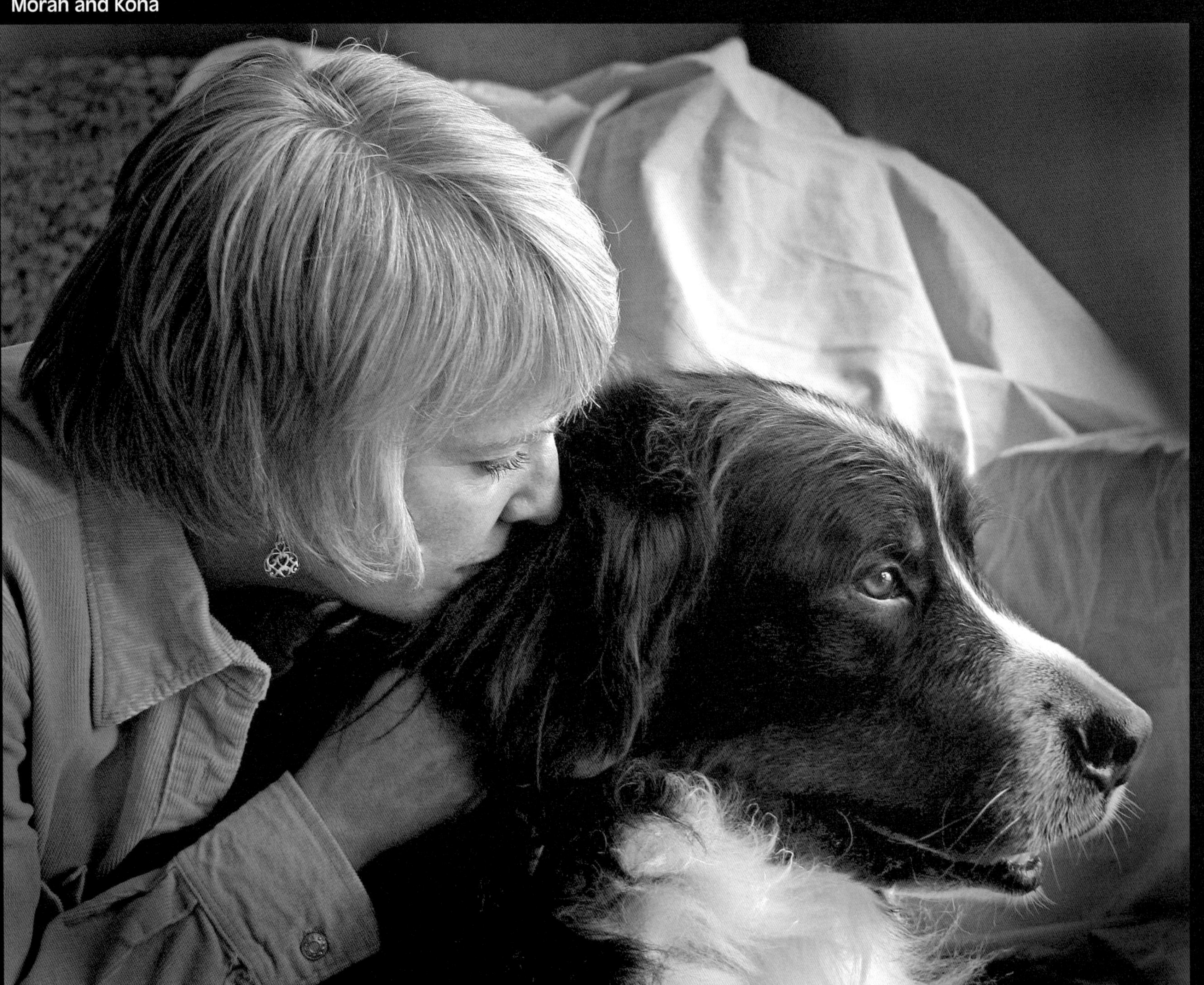

Kona demands nothing more than to be with me,

which suits me just fine.

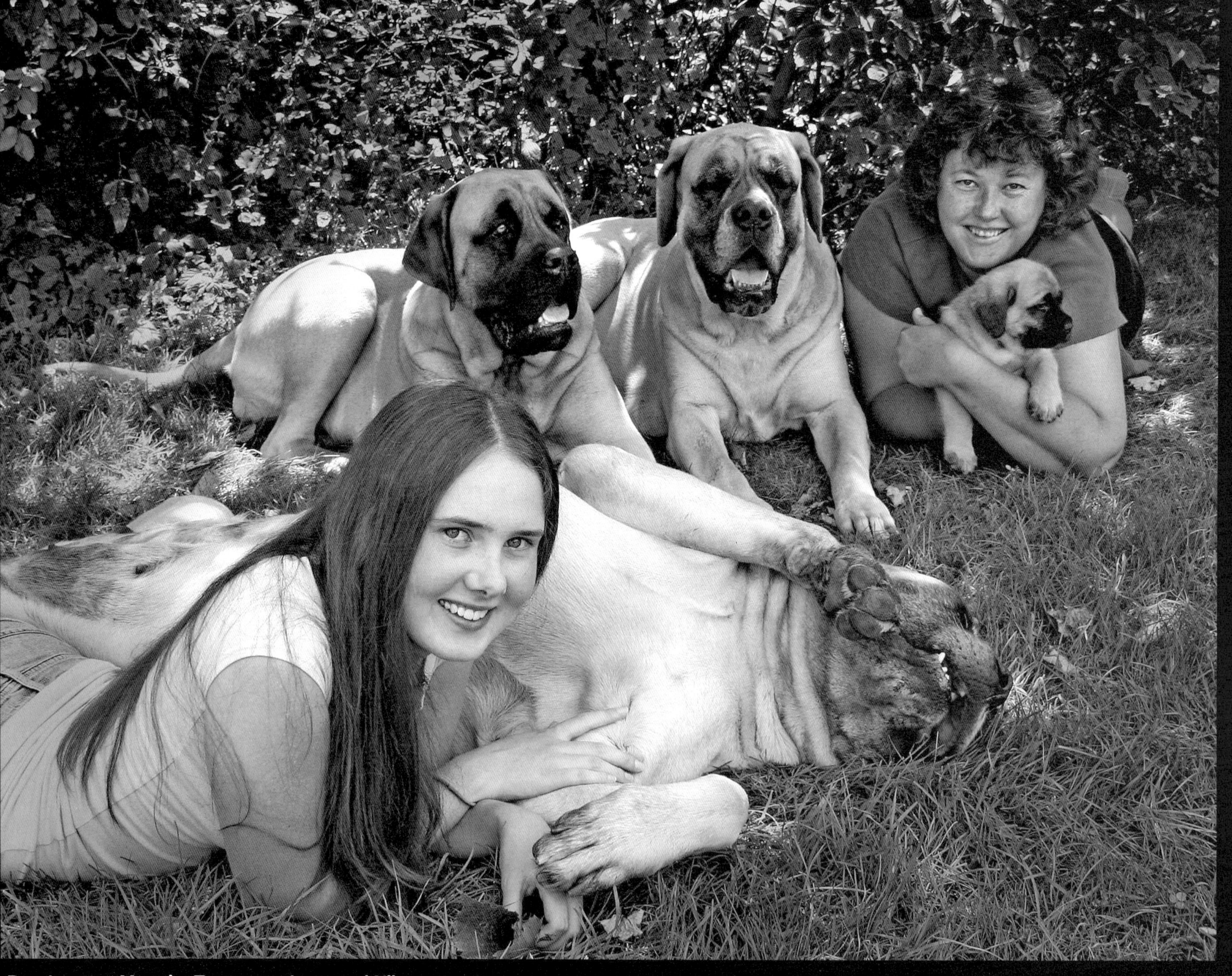

Bev, Lauren, Maggie, Tuppance, Lucy and Nike

Four generations of dogs and two generations of people.

We are one big happy family.

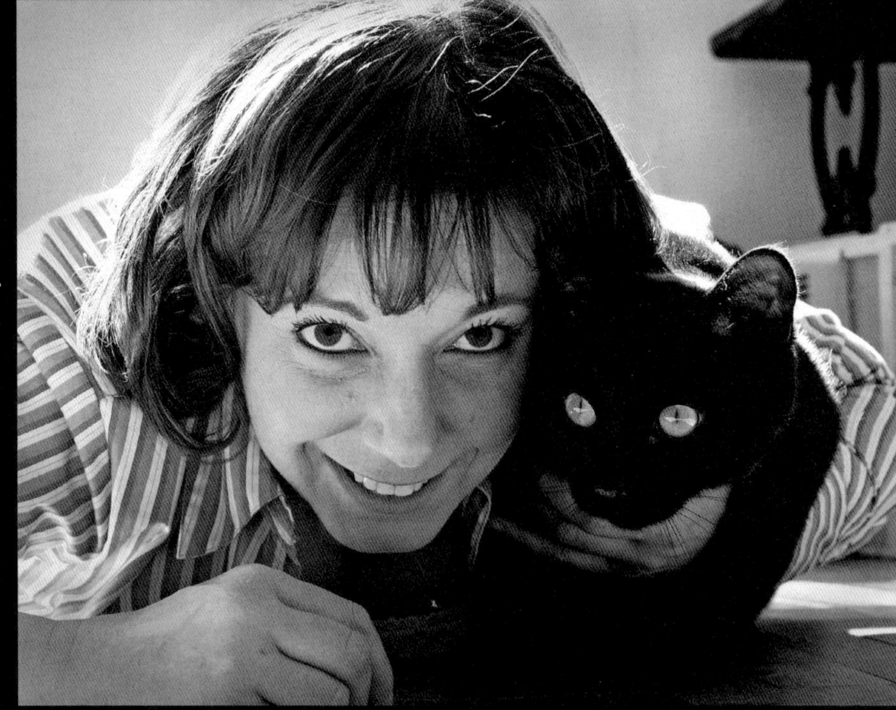



... And I thought I was strictly a dog lover!

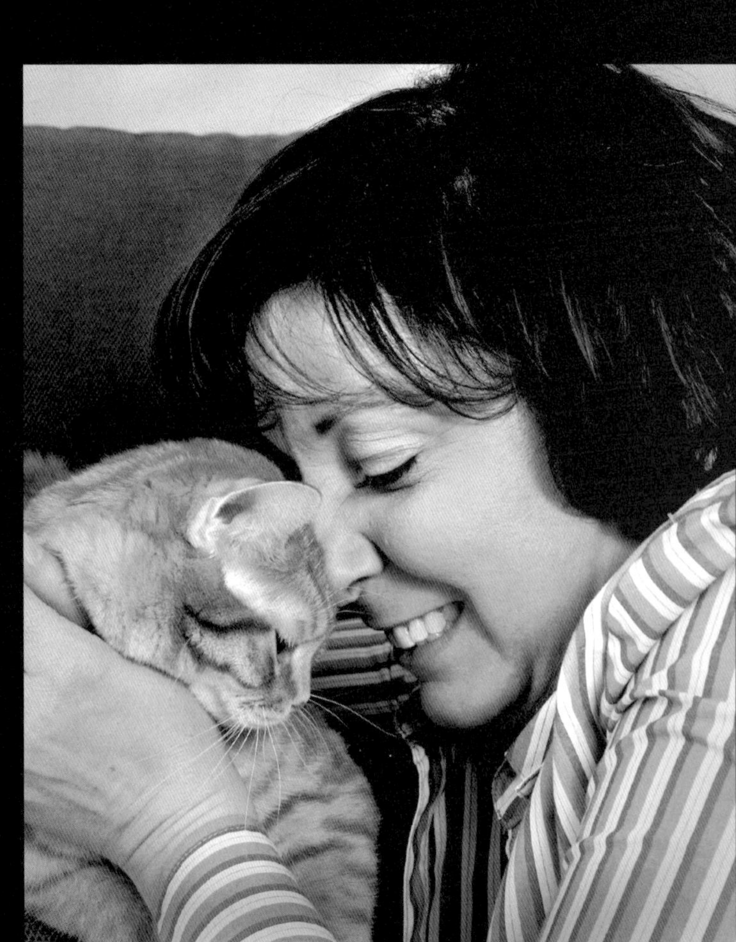

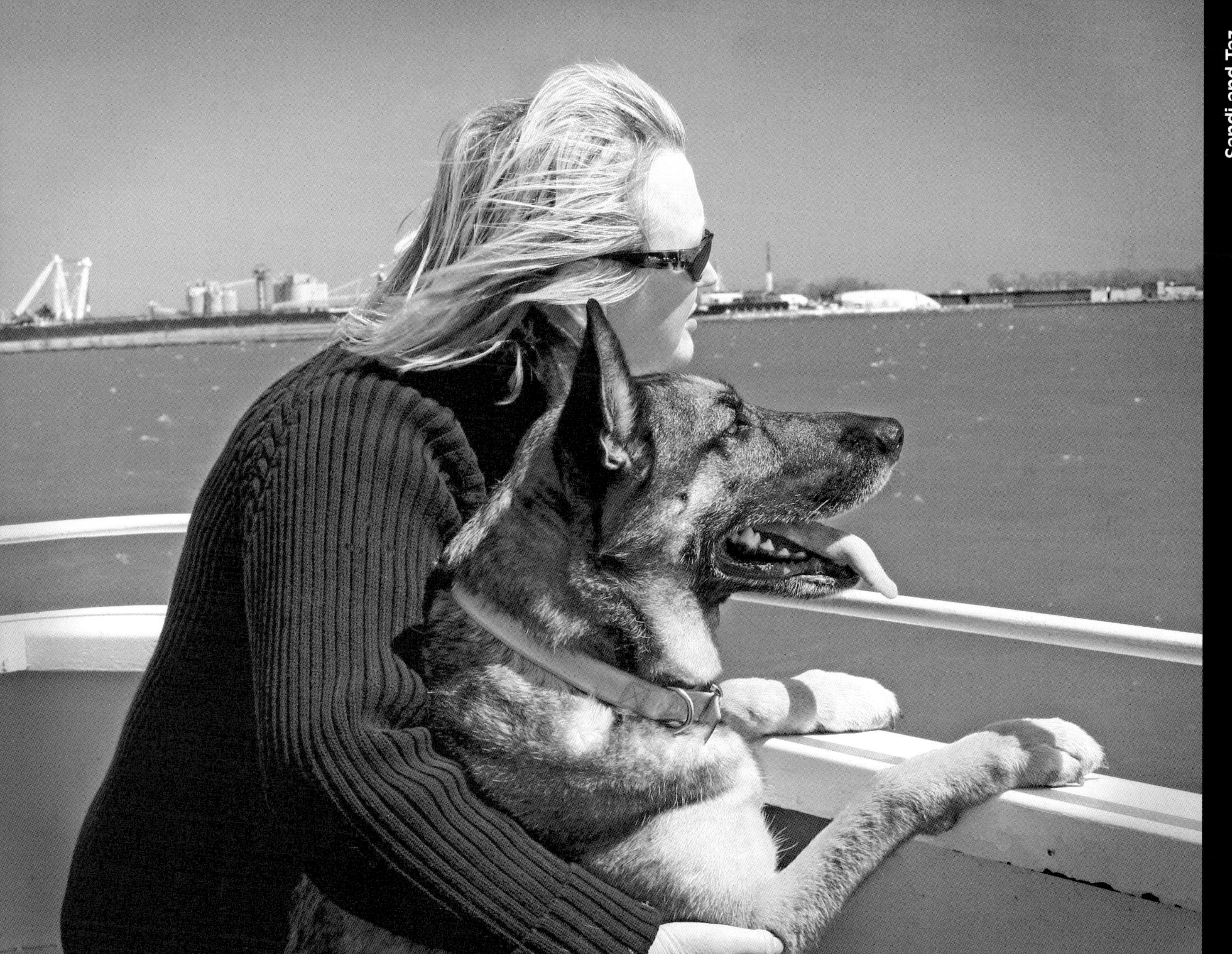
Sandi and Taz

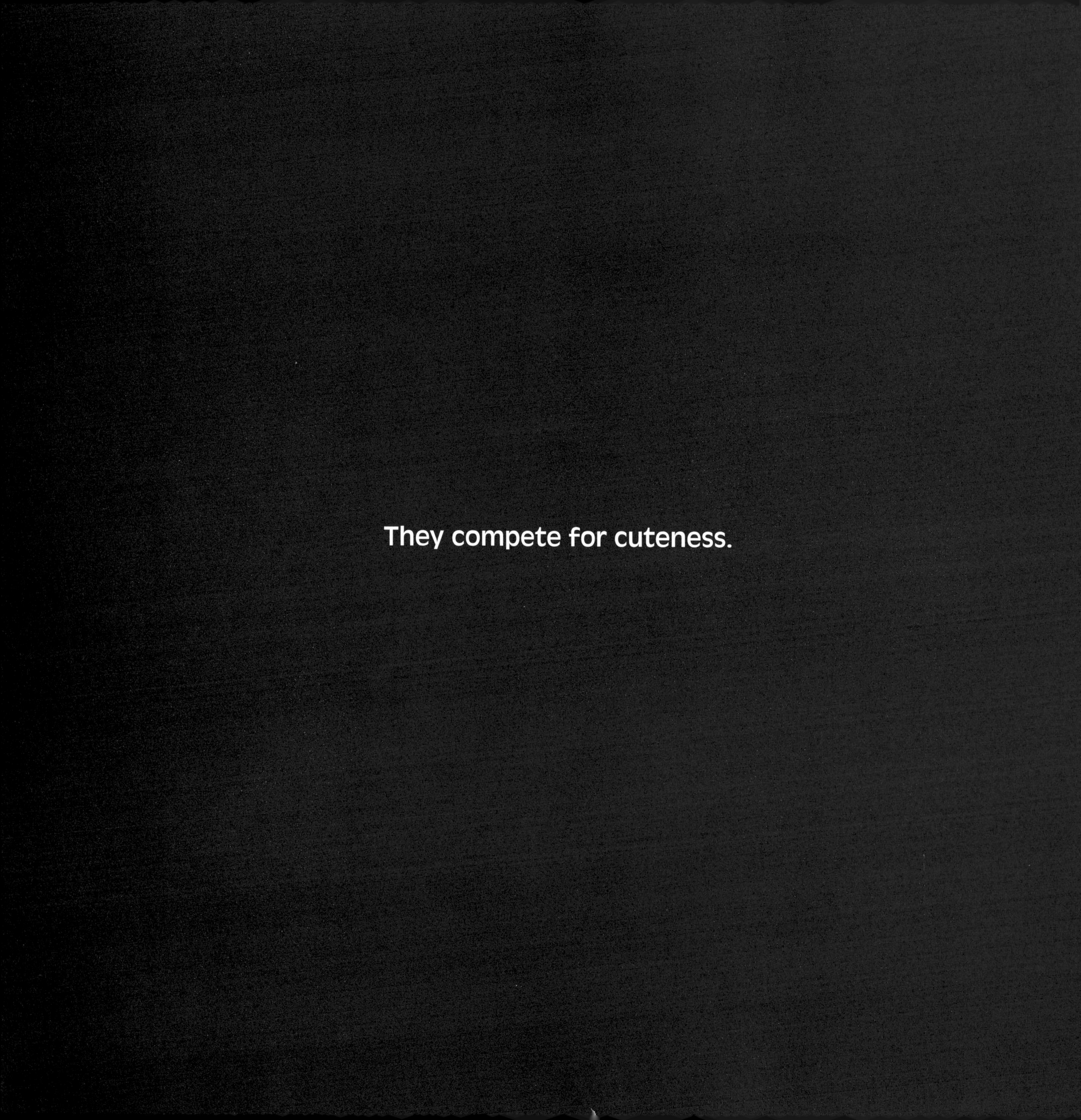

They compete for cuteness.

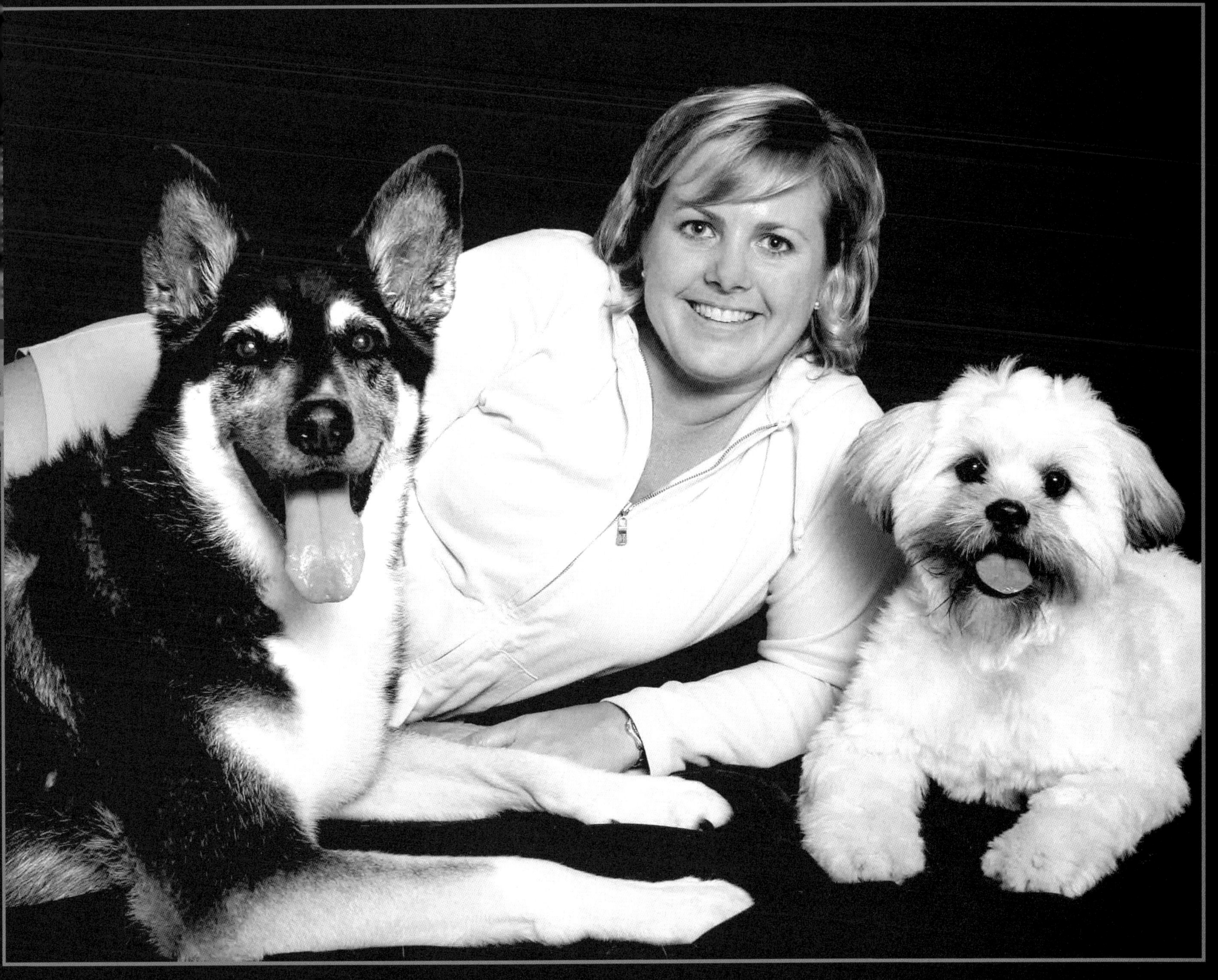

Larissa, Winston and Santo

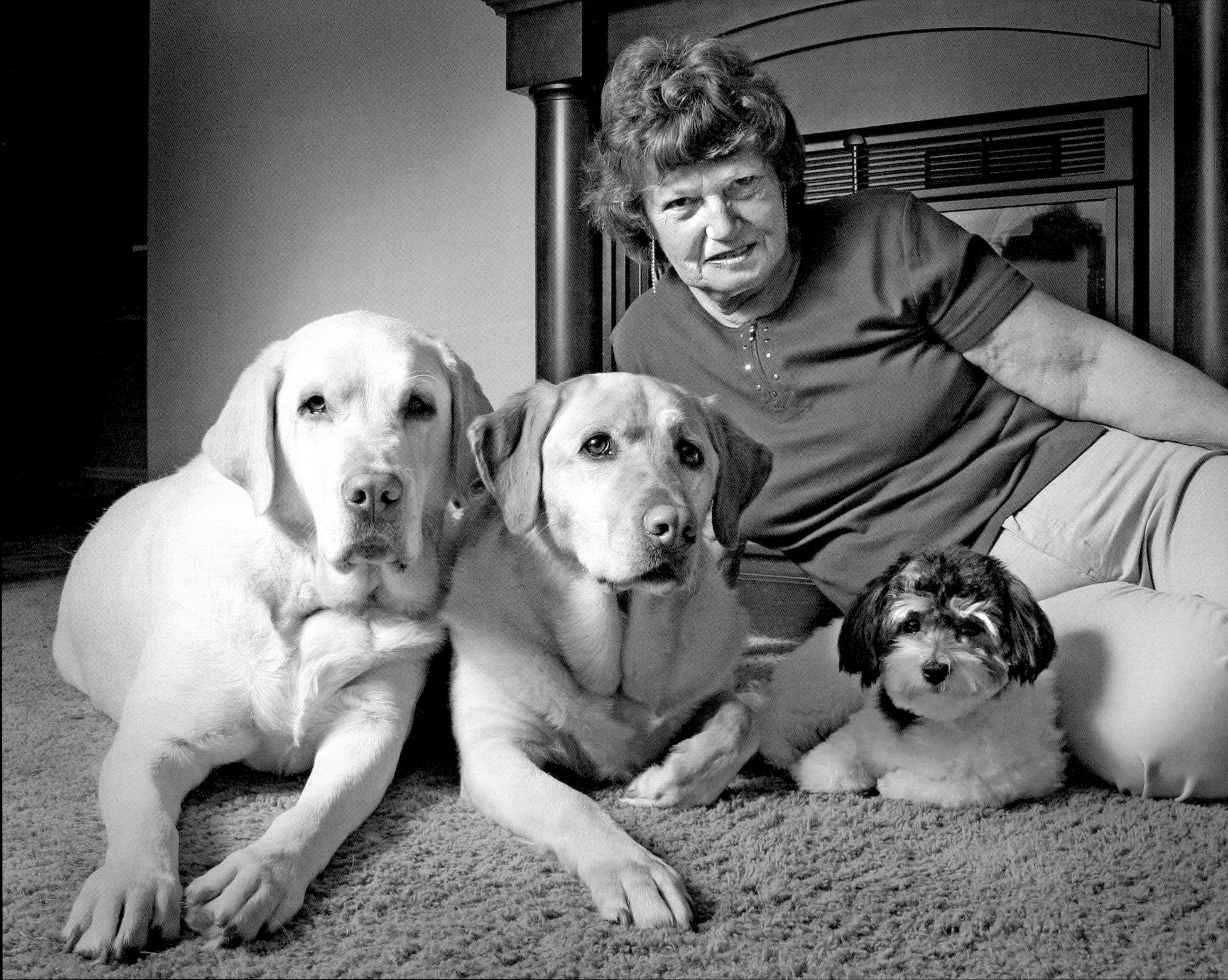

Gail, Indie, Draco and Saskee

Nobody kisses with more enthusiasm or with such sharp teeth.

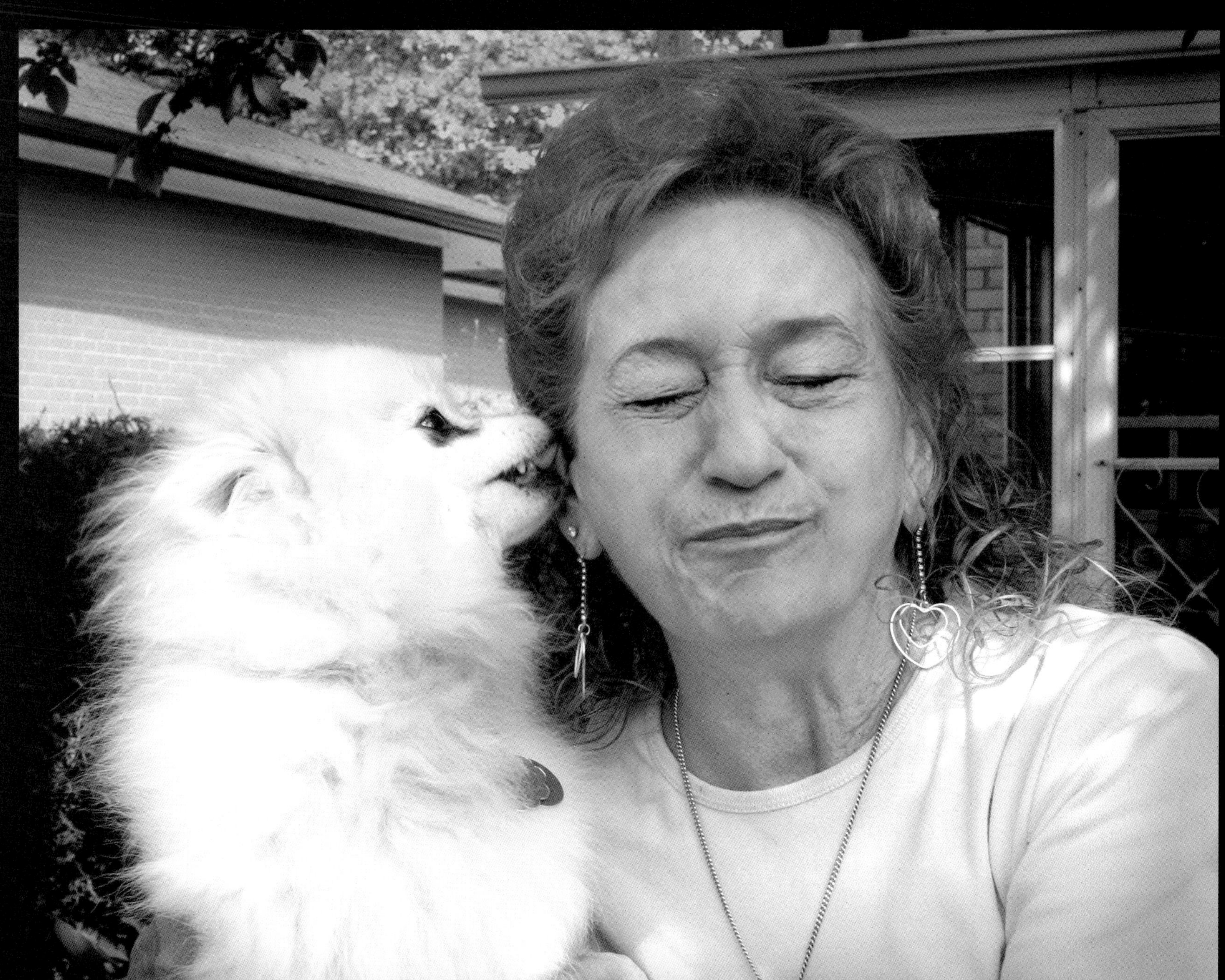

I may have bought Wellington,

but he owns me, heart and soul.

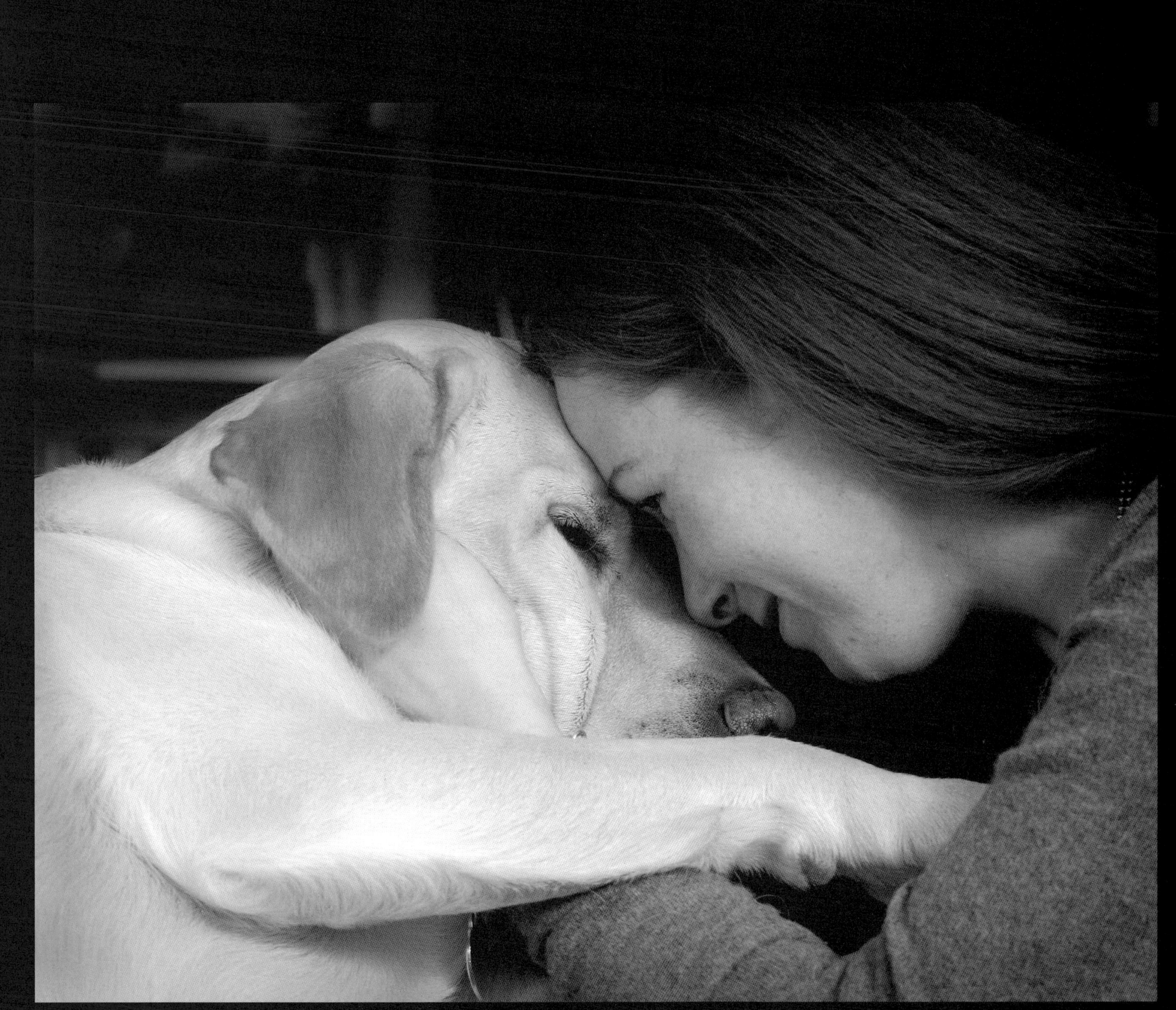

Erin and Wellington

Karen, Gracie, Georgie and Sophie

My three girls keep me going

because I know I have to be there for them,

just as they are always there for me.

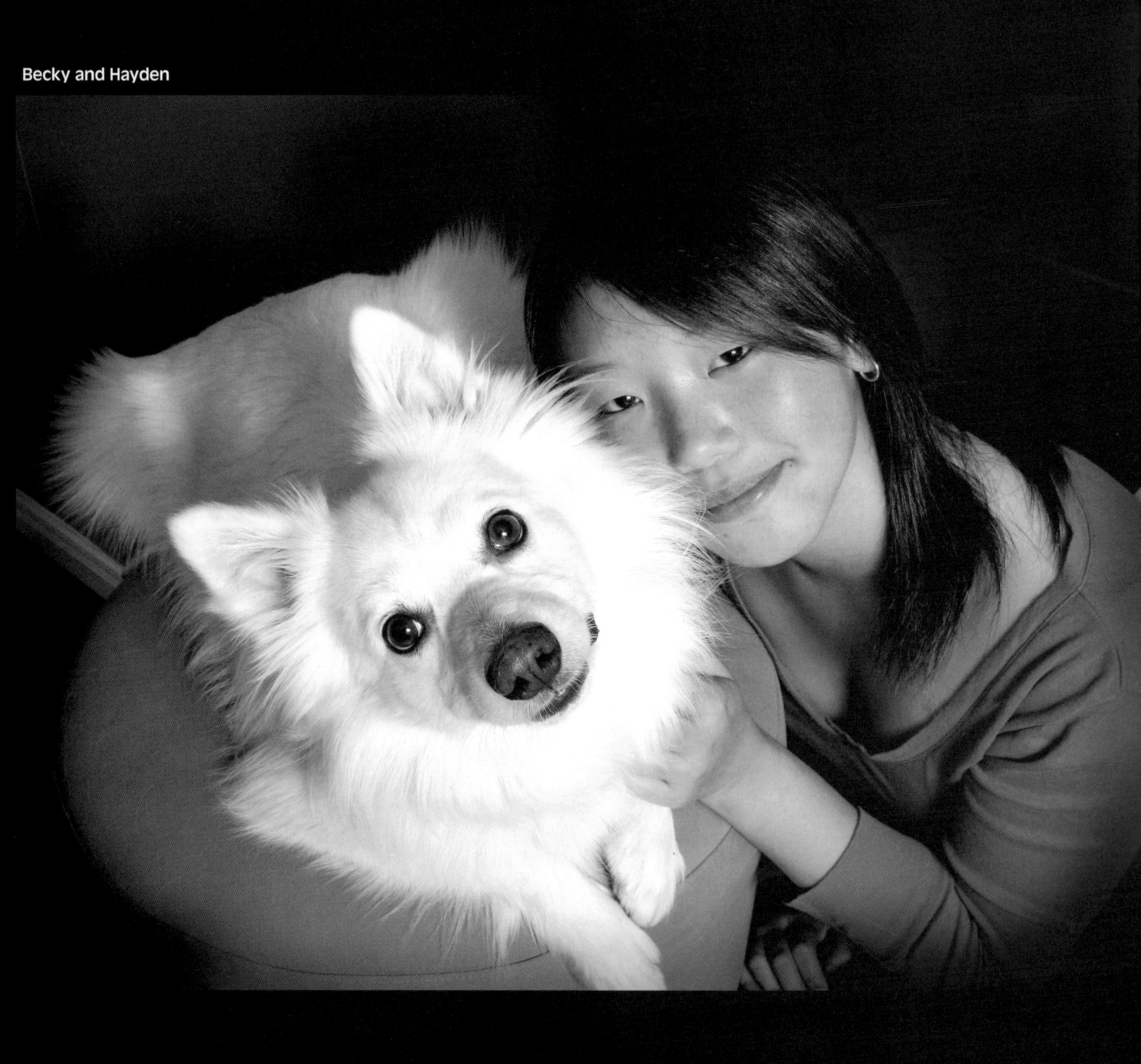
Becky and Hayden

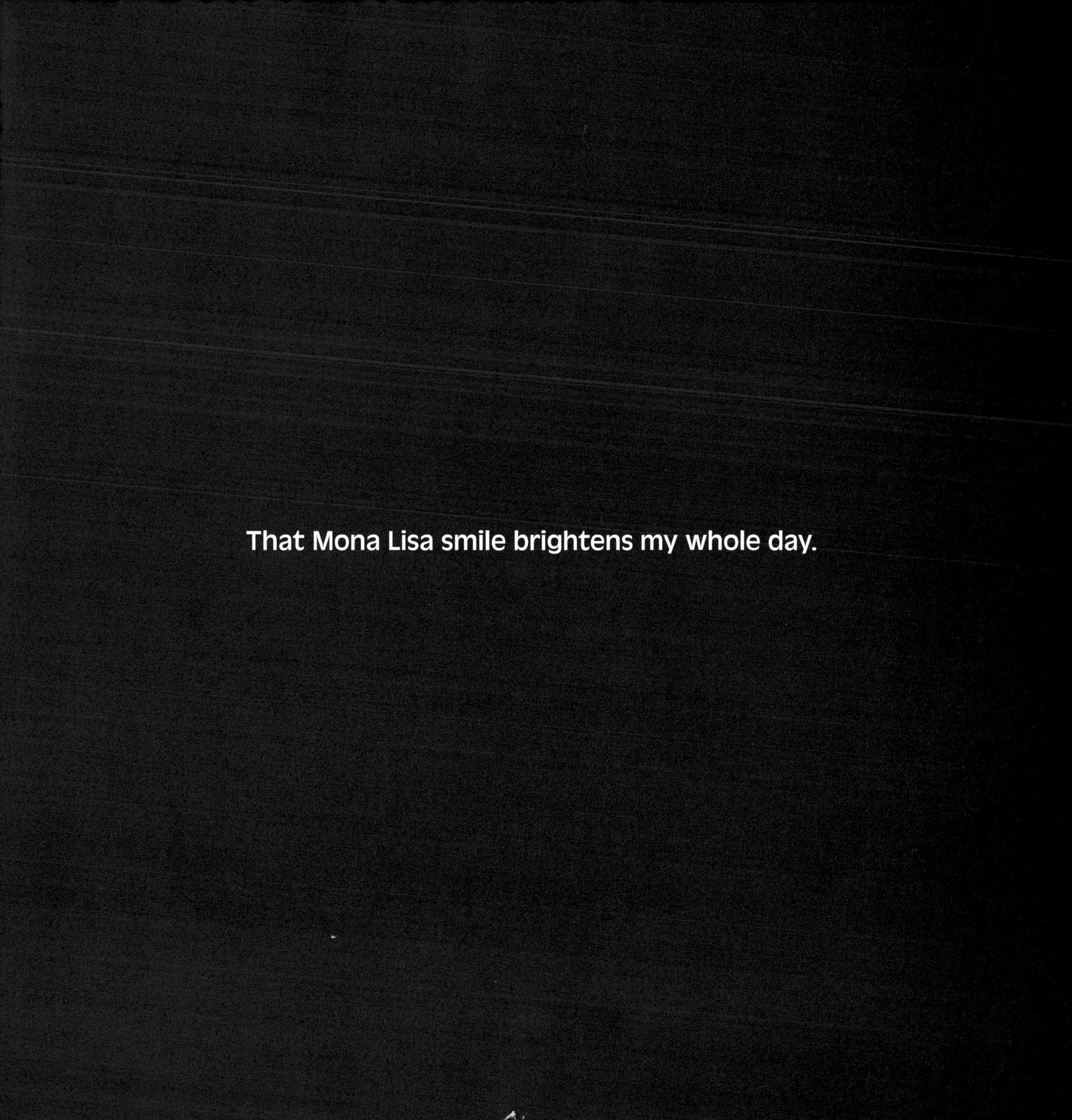

That Mona Lisa smile brightens my whole day.

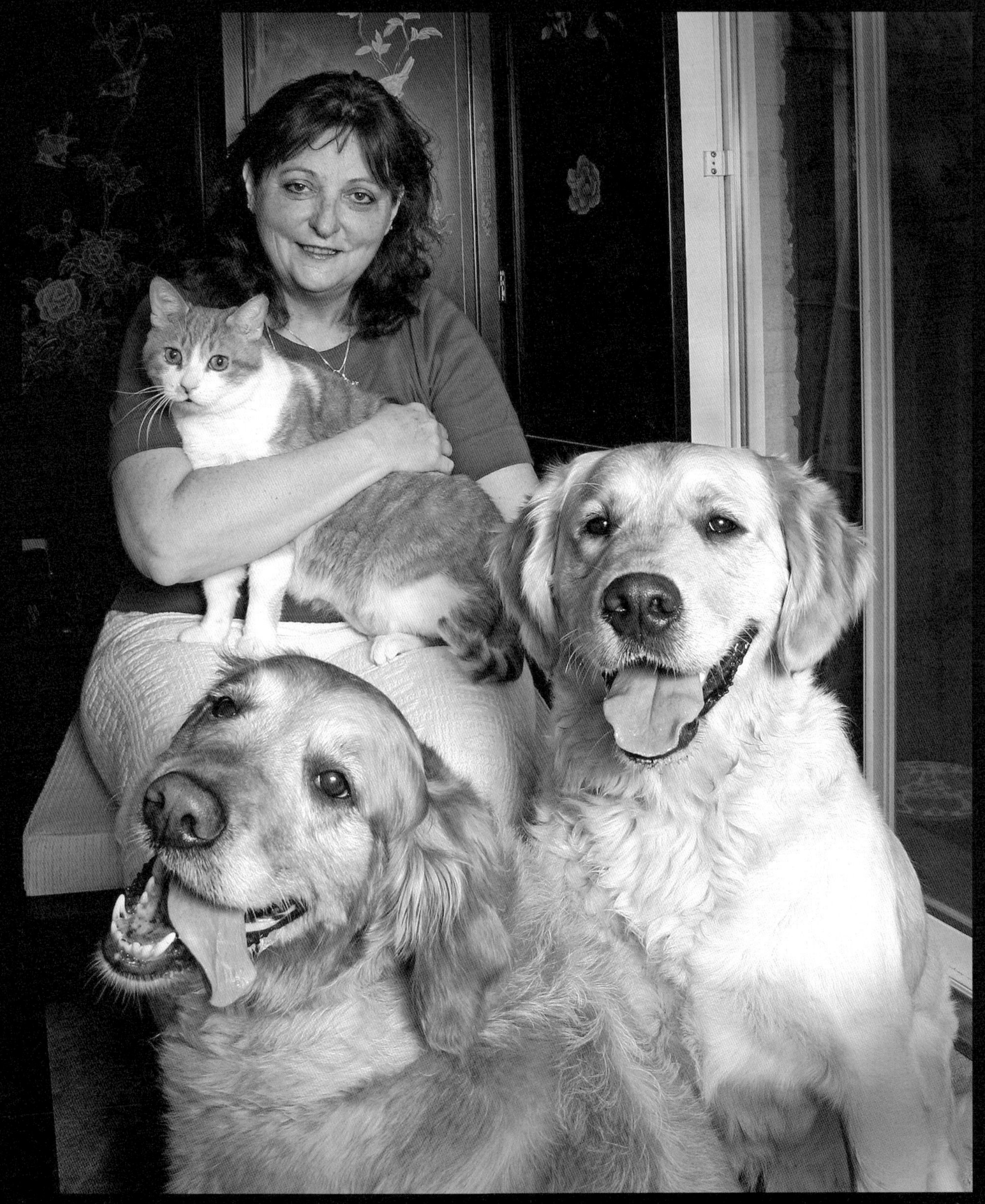



I think I said

"I don't want any

more pets!"

just before these

lovely creatures

arrived.

Now I can't

imagine life

without them.

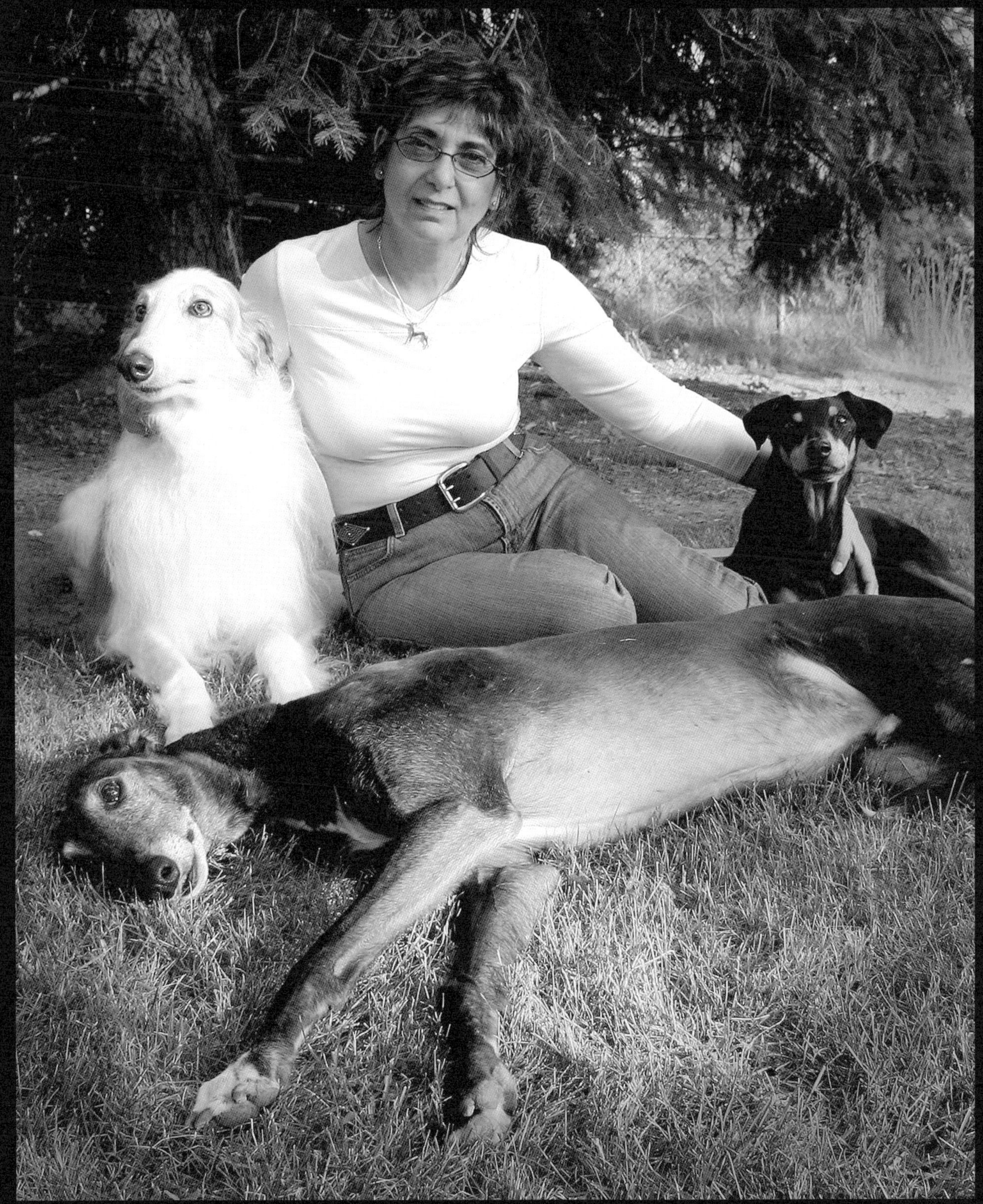

Rene, Zigi, Julian and Dmitri

I love the peacefulness that comes with being surrounded by my dogs.

Alice is a human trapped in a doggie suit;

Archie is my joker, my clown.

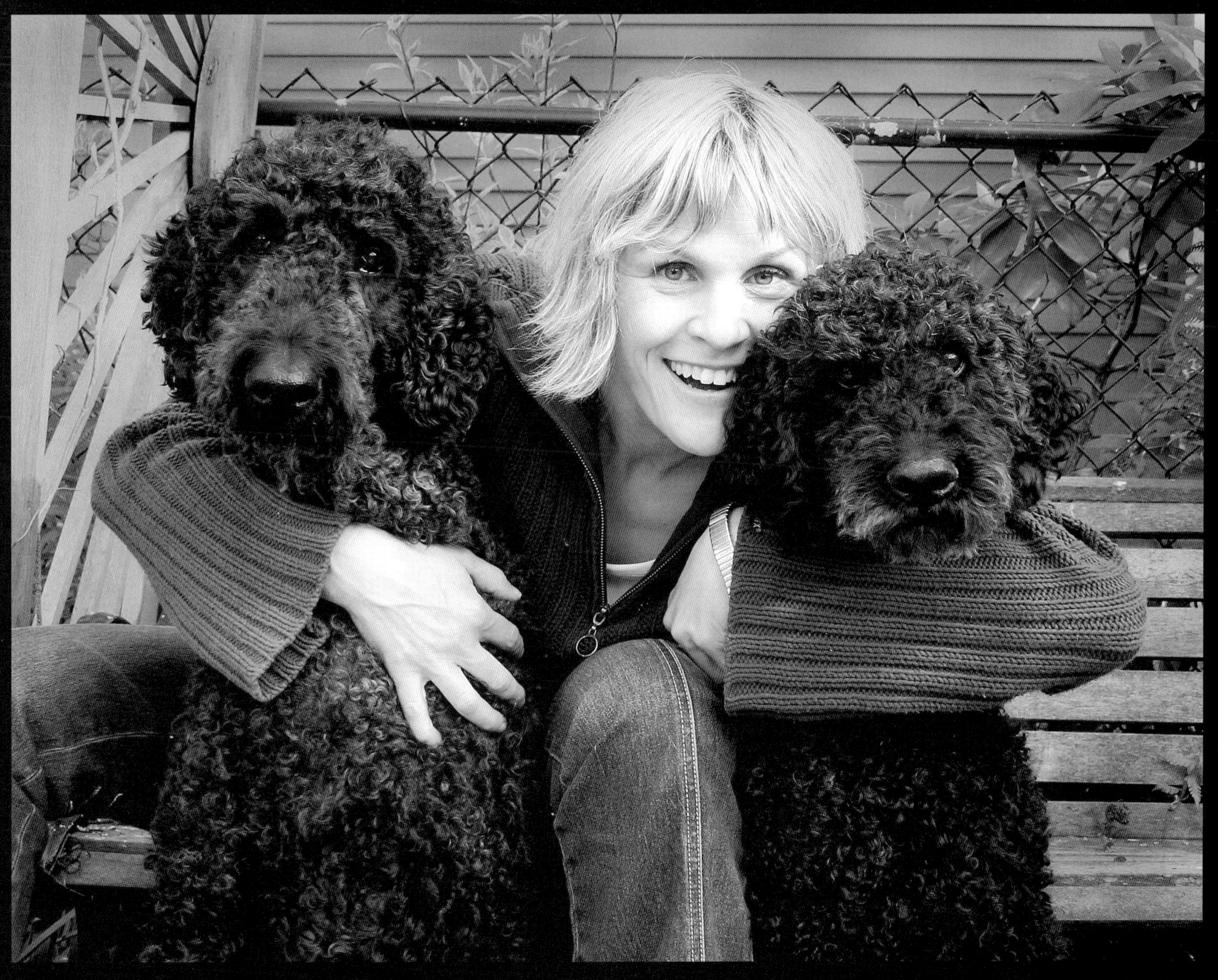

Linda, Alice and Archie

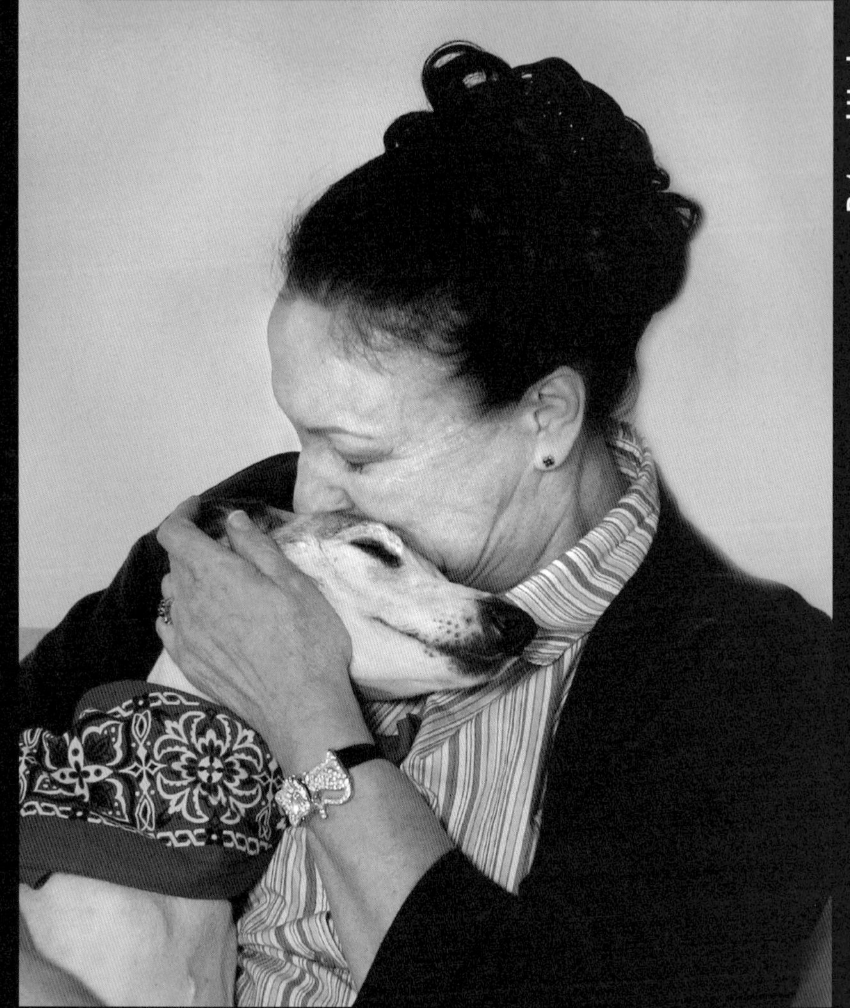


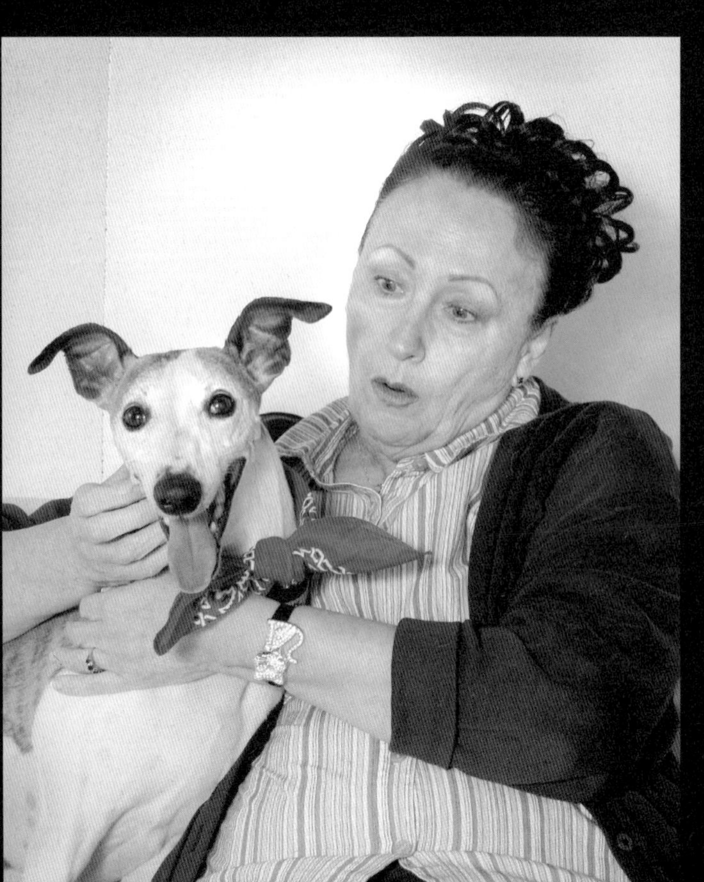

Harley sticks so close to me,

I should have named him "Velcro."

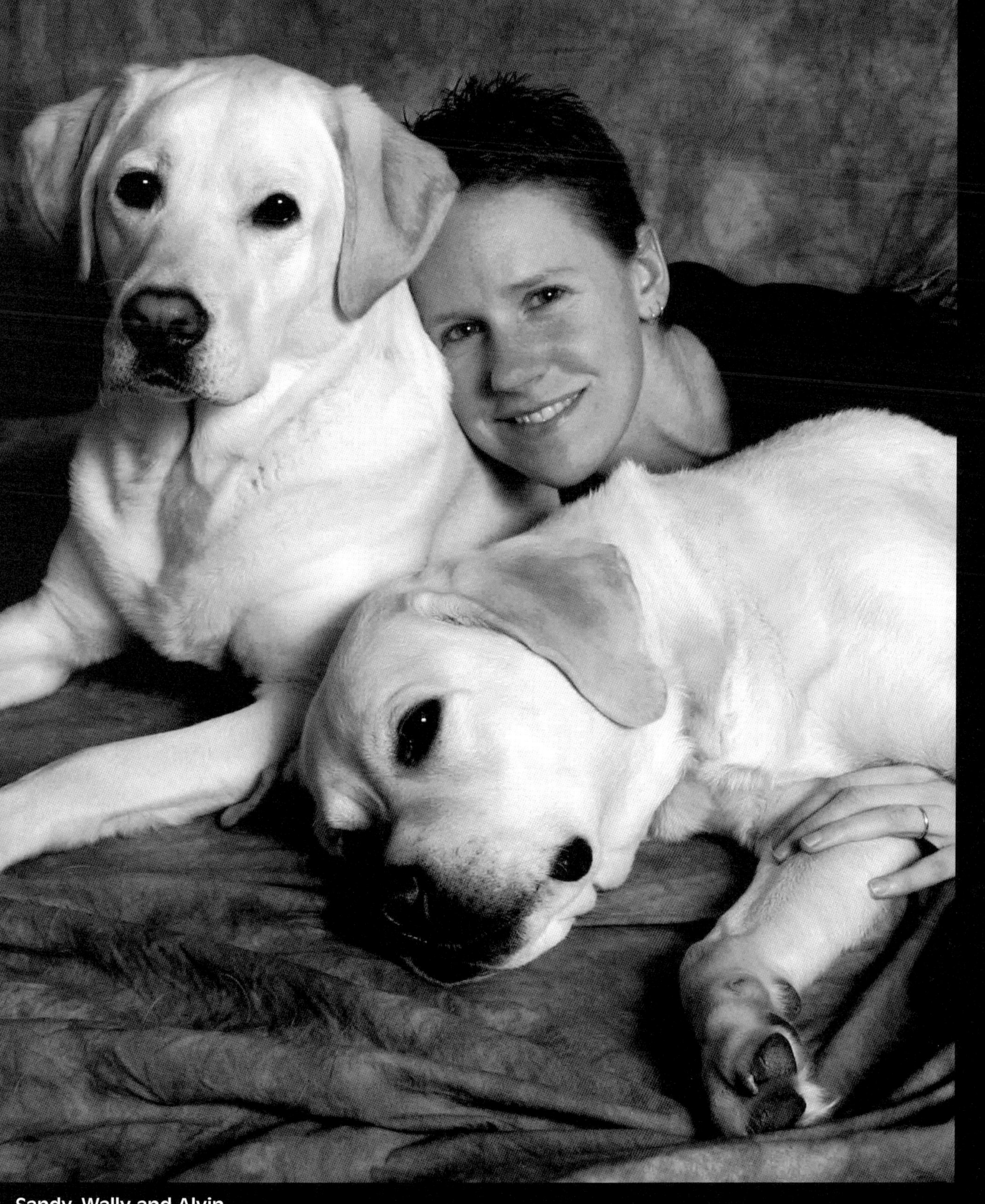



Sandy, Wally and Alvin

Sweet and loving, spunky and inquisitive.

And sometimes stubborn.

That's our Drake.

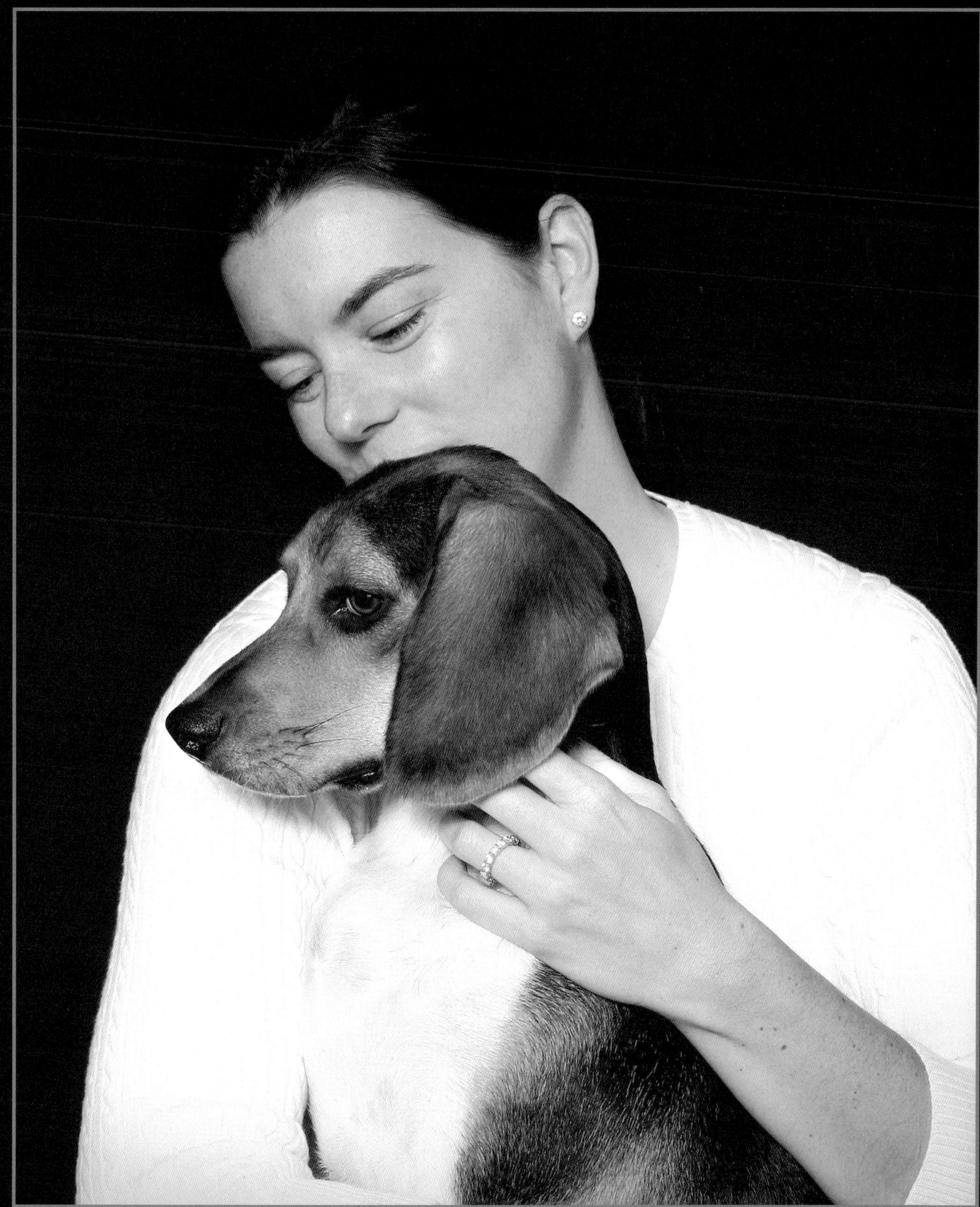

Sarah and Drake

## About the Author
A professional journalist and photographer for more than a decade, Sandra Bolan has
photographed everything from local tractor pulls and peewee hockey games to dignitaries and
historical events. But her favourite subject has always been animals. In 2001, she turned her lens on
the animal world and has had her photos published on greeting cards and in numerous magazines.
A Maxwell Award nominee, Sandra's first book, *Dogs and Dads*, received an Honourable Mention
award from the Independent Book Publishers Association.


## About the Editors
Jacque Newman is a three-time Maxwell Award winner, founder and former editor
of *Dogs, Dogs, Dogs!*

Brian Balogh has been in the photography industry for more than a decade.

# Mail Order Coupon

Please send me ______ copies of Dogs and Dads @ $19.95 each  _____________

Please send me ______ copies of Moms and Paws @ $22.95 each _____________

Postage and handling: $3 for the first book, $1 for each additional book.

Canadian residents add 6% GST  _____________

TOTAL AMOUNT ENCLOSED  _____________

Enclosed is my ☐ cheque  ☐ money order

## Mailing Information

Name _________________________________________________________

Address ____________________________________________________

City ____________________ Province ___________ Postal Code___________

If this is a gift, please provide your contact information, as well as the recipient's name and mailing address.

Please make all cheques or money orders payable to Fetch it Up!

Mail to:
Fetch It Up!
646 Walpole Cres.
Newmarket, Ontario
L3X 2B4